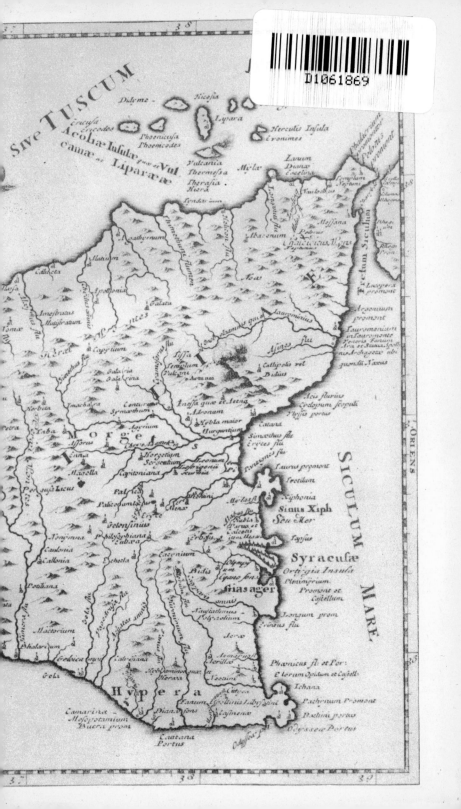

SPRING IN SICILY

To Daphne and Whitney Straight

I *PALERMO: Fountain in the Piazza Pretoria*

SPRING
IN SICILY

by

PETER QUENNELL

ILLUSTRATIONS BY JOAN RAYNER
AND OTHERS

GEORGE WEIDENFELD
AND NICOLSON LIMITED
7 Cork Street, London, W.1

First published in 1952
by George Weidenfeld & Nicolson Limited
7 Cork Street, London, W.1

Printed by
Co-operative Wholesale Society Limited
South Reddish, Stockport

Contents

List of Illustrations

ACKNOWLEDGEMENTS

My thanks are due to The Cresset Press for permission to reprint 12 lines from *Archaic Marble Sculpture From The Acropolis* by Humfry Payne and Gerard Mackworth Young; to Messrs. William Heinemann for permission to reprint 11 lines from *Mainly On The Air* by Sir Max Beerbohm; to Messrs. Bruno Cassirer for permission to reproduce the photograph of the coin appearing opposite page 17 from *Masterpieces of Greek Coinage* by Charles Seltman; to Consociazione Turistica Italiana for permission to reproduce the illustrations numbered 2, 3, 5, 6, 7, 8, 13, 16, 18, 19, 20 and 22 from *Sicilia*. The photograph of the terra-cotta head (plate 21) was taken by Messrs. Gee & Watson.

I

ACROSS SICILY THE clouds were mountainous,
an Alpine landscape of moving vapours, precipices piled high
overhead—the shadow of the plane, rainbow-encircled, flitting
past along the cloud-walls—and huge chasms which opened on
to sudden glimpses of dark, forlorn, mysterious country. Immediately below appeared a wintry hill-town, its yellow tile roofs,
dusted and rimmed with snow, tightly conglomerated round the
sepulchral chink of a narrow empty main square. Melancholy the
associations of that cold town and the native life it represented.
Between tall buildings, shuttered and self-absorbed, black-cloaked
and black-shawled inhabitants must be going silently about their
business, everywhere black figures against grey or yellowish
masonry. Sicily, I began to remember, has two contrasted aspects.
There is the gaiety of the coastal fringe, particularly on the east
and south-west, in which flowers are plentiful, colours are bright,
and radiant traces of Hellenic civilisation still glitter on the limestone rocks; and there is the severity of the inland districts and
the seaside towns of the extreme west, where another civilisation
has left its deposit, speech is reserved and faces are sombre, and

the swinging cloaks of secretive villagers suggest perpetual mourning—just such an air of traditional gloom as seemed to be hinted at by the hill-town far below me.

Then Etna gradually emerged, most delightful of volcanic peaks, with which years ago I had often compared, and always greatly to their disadvantage, the curves of Fujiyama. Through the dim whiteness of surging and shifting cloud shone the marble gleam of snowfields. I had admired the crest and a part of the shoulder when the downward sweep of the plane took us into cloud again. Etna's crest had completely vanished; but beneath cloud-level the whole gigantic terrain, brown and dusky olive-green, patched with orchards and vineyards, seamed with pallid serpentine water-courses, rose tilting up towards it. Invisible Etna commanded the prospect; for every contour, as it approached the mountain, had a slowly climbing tendency, a purposeful upward swing which merged into the foothills. We turned right and Etna receded. It was chilly twilight, and the sea was glassy smooth, as we wheeled above Augusta.

Temporary stopping places are usually dismal; and Augusta, although Etna shines in the distance, and it has a magnificently scooped-out natural anchorage and an airship hangar which, during the war, some ingenious strategist decided to camouflage as the largest of Greek temples, is scarcely more interesting than Dover, Calais, Modane. Passengers to Karachi dismount from the launch and, with commiseratory glances at the fellow-passenger said to be getting off here, hurry away under solicitous escort in the direction of the new hotel. But Augusta possesses the advantage of being close to Syracuse; and, for a traveller who hopes to explore Sicily, there is no better jumping-off point. Syracuse is ancient and compact and small. It saw the defeat of the noblest of Greek democracies, whose hubristic aspirations collapsed within its spacious harbour: it was the home of a

curiously inspired tyrant, who dug his memorials, hundreds of
feet deep, into the rocky hill behind it. Syracuse, moreover, is a
city with a strongly individual life; even its present shape is
remarkable, linked to the mainland by an exiguous isthmus and
built upon an island-peninsula not unlike a duck's head. The head
of the bird is called Ortygia; and here the original colony was
founded, and the various masters of Syracuse had their arsenals
and palaces. But, beyond the neck, sprawls the modern town and,
considerably beyond and above its untidy modern suburbs,
extended the old settlements of Tycha and Achradina, walled
and densely populated, with theatres, temples and civic buildings.
To-day the focus of the city is the island itself, a wedge of buff-
coloured stone incorporating the architecture and sculptured
ornament of half a dozen periods.

The Cathedral, for instance, in the elegant Piazza del Duomo,
belongs both to the fifth century before, and the eighteenth
century after, Christ. Originally a shrine of Athene, whose gilded
shield, flashing far out to sea, was displayed upon the pediment,
it is said to have been remodelled as a Christian church by a
certain Bishop Zosimus in the seventh century; but not until the
seventeen-twenties did a Syracusan, Pompeo Picherati, begin to
raise his new façade, a sumptuous achievement of southern
baroque, designed in the boldest traditions of architectural
rhetoric. Behind this exuberant screen, the sober classical prose
of Doric columns is built into the church walls. The *cella* of the
temple is the body of the cathedral; and here, soon after I had
arrived in Syracuse, when taking refuge from the cold spring
wind, I was temporarily laid low by a tremendous sermon, which
just at that moment I neither wanted nor expected. Before two
mitred ecclesiastics—white mitre and yellow-and-red mitre, each
parchment-wrinkled and resignedly decrepit among swarthy,
blue-chinned ministrants—a black-and-white Dominican friar

was rolling forth his periods, raising his deep sleeves with compulsive gestures and now and then disengaging a hand to thrust some painful point home. His were the movements of an excited politician in any Sicilian or South-Italian meeting-place —palm exhibited, fingers extended, then snapped emphatically together as if to seize a floating thread—yet vibrant with an urgency that even politics could not have given them; for his subject was the imminence of death, the calm death of the virtuous Catholic in contrast to the anguished and terror-stricken passing of the materialist or free-thinker, who in the supreme crisis of mortal existence must be deprived of *every* hope, of *every* shade of spiritual comfort . . .

"*Ogni speranza! Ogni conforto!*"—his voice rose to a booming taurine bellow, sank to a low and harsh, but penetrating, whisper. By comparison how quiet and smooth, how orderly and regular and decent was the extinction of the good man! And, almost voluptuously, he appeared to stroke the air, as though he intended to illustrate the soul's gentle heavenward progress, seeking eternal security after a brief sojourn in realms of sin and turmoil. Meanwhile coloured mitre sat calm and stolid, white mitre fidgeted irritably at his stiff and heavy vestments. An elderly congregation crouched dusky and silent; and the nerve-racked sceptic in the shelter of a column tried to escape from thoughts of annihilation by surreptitious sight-seeing. The interior of the Cathedral is dull and plain enough. But supposing, like the letters of a palimpsest disclosed beneath more modern script, some shadowy impression of its pagan splendour were to emerge above the bishop's throne—the head and breastplate of Athene herself, since her effigy must have been situated near the modern altar-rails . . . What were her appurtenances, and what the decorations that filled her shrine and outer sanctuary? We can trace the skeleton of a Greek or Roman temple; but the imagination of the sightseer can never quite reclothe the bones, supplying the innumerable votive statues and dedicated temple-furniture, the tripods and the vases and the celebrated pictures collected by the priesthood. Syracusan shrines were particularly rich in sacerdotal art-collections; and the temple of Athene, besides its chryselephantine doors, with "minutely executed" ivory panels, contained a series of pictures, covering the inner walls, which represented a cavalry-engagement of the Syracusan king Agathocles. Famed among Hellenistic art-critics, these paintings were afterwards looted by a notorious Roman governor.

What Verres did in his clumsy *parvenu* fashion, a long line of subsequent enemies of beauty—Saracenic, Byzantine, Norman—have done with even greater thoroughness. The treasures of Syracuse have melted away; and the Museum, not far from the Cathedral, contains the mutilated fragments of only two distinguished statues. Each is the torso of a young man, one archaic, the other of the early fifth century; and, whereas there is an exquisite formalism about the earlier statue—the lines of the body flattened and elongated, an ideal rhythm superimposed upon the artist's knowledge of the actual fleshly structure—in the second the archaic convention is losing its rigidity, though its influence can still be felt, checking any hint of exuberance, giving an air of dignified reserve to this gravely steadfast athlete. Head, arms and legs have been broken off; but such was the restrained, and yet romantic, tenderness with which the artist represented him—dwelling on the narrow compact hips, the straight back, the broad, but by no means heavy or over-muscular, shoulders—that loss of limbs and identity has involved no loss of personality. The work is "classical" in the noblest sense of the word; a lively appreciation of the charm of the living flesh co-exists with a resolute aversion from emotionalism for its own sake; emergent naturalism nowhere degenerates into vulgar realism. The effect, nevertheless, is delicately sensuous—how coolly and chastely sensuous, if one compares these two male statues, produced in the spring of Greek art, with a product of its tired and sultry autumn, the renowned and atrocious Aphrodite, dug up at the beginning of the last century by an archaeologist named Landolina! Maupassant, whose narrative gifts seem today as remarkable as the accompanying strain of tastelessness, saw the Aphrodite when he visited Syracuse and voiced his admiration of it. *Une belle femme* indeed!—almost as good as the real thing and, since "the gloomy bull", an indefatigable lover, appears to have experienced constant pangs of disillusionment, from the literary point of view a yet more satisfying cult-object. The marble, he declared, was really alive. "*On le voudrait palper avec la certitude qu'il cédera sous la main, comme de la chair . . . C'est un corps de femme qui exprime toute la poésie réelle de la caresse.*" Certainly the marble looks as if it would yield to the touch; there is a surprising verisimilitude in the deep-carved dimples of those over-generous haunches; but poetry is an attribute that we can no longer claim for them. The earlier sculptors conferred on flesh the solid grace of marble, without losing the charm of the transient fleshly envelope; the Hellenistic craftsman imposed on stone all the banality of the living organism—of a stout *hetaira* who emerges from the bath and, with a practised gesture of immodest modesty, attempts to gather up her fallen robes . . .

Syracuse, however, is not properly to be enjoyed in its museums or its churches. It is a place for walking and staring—for sitting on walls, craning at windows, and peering into open doors. Nearly opposite the Cathedral, a little to the right of it, the Palazzo Beneventano del Bosco is a gay yet urbane achievement of early eighteenth-century architecture. But every street, particularly towards the tip of the island, is lined with former palaces now more or less dilapidated, Gothic or Saracenic Gothic,

Renaissance, High Baroque, with well-proportioned garden-courts and processional outer staircases, scutcheoned *portes cochères* and bulging wrought-iron balconies, poised over the pavement on heavily-sculptured stone brackets. The sea is never far away, and most of my walks around Syracuse eventually took me there, either to the east side of Ortygia, approached by narrow crumbling back-lanes, much encumbered with talkative family-groups, squatting on rush-bottomed chairs, their feet among the poultry: or to the western face of the peninsula which looks across the Great Harbour. Rising above the massive sea-wall, the tall buildings of the city form a long continuous bastion; and Syracuse from this angle assumes a look of pride and consequence, the expression of a metropolis that, since the eighth century before Christ, when Corinthian settlers first established it, has had a record of unbroken activity, though frequently besieged and on several occasions taken and plundered, while ancient Corinth completely disappeared, and Athens herself once dwindled into an obscure Turkish village.

Out of the rock of the foreshore bubbles Arethusa's fountain. The tutelary nymph of Syracuse, according to a rather perplexing legend, came originally from Arcadia, pursued by the river god Alpheus with whose stream she had refused to marry. But her fresh springs mingle with the salt of the sea; and on the many exquisite coins that display her likeness dolphins plunge and weave among the serpentine intricacies of Arethusa's unbound hair. A typically Hellenic stroke of imagination. For, however sensitive to the splendour of the natural world, a Greek was constantly re-interpreting it in terms of human beauty. A river was a graceful young man, or, if it were one of those Southern torrents which suddenly swell to a bellowing flood and tumultuously override their banks, a human-headed bull, half-grotesque and half-majestic. Arethusa was an elusive virgin, whose attraction

remains constant but whose face varies with the period. During
the earlier part of the fifth century, in coins struck by "the
Demareteion Master," she is almost Asiatic, with a long fine
nose, delicately prominent lips and a large lustrous heavily-lidded
eye. But then, upon these coins the head of Arethusa is said to be
a royal portrait, reproducing the features of Queen Demarete,
wife of Gelon, tyrant of Syracuse, sister to his ally Theron, the
warrior prince of Akragas. A year earlier Gelon and Theron had
defeated an invading Carthaginian army at the battle of Himera;
and Demarete is reputed to have pleaded with her husband and
her brother to grant the Carthaginians easy terms. The grateful
enemy gave her a golden diadem, which Demarete sold, trans-
forming the proceeds of the sale into silver coinage. That a
Syracusan queen should have adopted the cause of the defeated
Carthaginians—themselves merciless in victory—seems a little
puzzling. Is it possible that she was of partly Phoenician descent,
offspring of some distinguished prisoner-of-war, captured in an
earlier campaign? Certainly she has a look of Astarte—or of a
princess-priestess dedicated to the service of an ancient hieratic
cult—rather than the sensuous candour of an unsophisticated
Grecian water-nymph.

The design of the Demareteion was executed by some unknown
genius in the year 479 before the Christian era. His successors,
Euainetos, Kimon and other famous journeymen-artists, who
travelled to and fro among the Grecian city states, sometimes
working in Sicily, sometimes in South Italy, engraving gems and
designing dies for coins and exercising their talent upon ivory,
bronze and precious metals, had completely shaken off any traces
of exotic or archaic influence. Their Arethusa is a Hellenic girl
—either the proud and voluptuous creature whom Euainetos
represented, as it might be the pampered consort of some rich
Sicilian citizen, viewed in profile with heavy ear-ring and fringed

2 *SYRACUSE: The Cathedral*

3 SYRACUSE: *Ortygia from the air*

4 *HEAD OF ARETHUSA by Kimon on a Syracusan coin of the fifth century*

and jewelled hair-band: or Kimon's marvellous full-faced head, probably the loveliest work of its kind ever conceived and carried out in Europe. Here is the nymph as we should like to remember her; her face is softly moulded; her eyes are large and alive; and the metallic bulk of the plunging dolphins—the wild dolphins of the Mediterranean, who run exultantly ahead of a storm and leap and weave about the ship's prow—is in fascinating contrast to the fine-spun curls of hair by which they are surrounded.

Arethusa's fountain today is neatly walled and railed off. It fills a large circular pool, sunk beneath the street-level, where papyrus plants grow, carp swim and a couple of parti-coloured geese pursue an existence of energetic leisure. When I saw them, they were welcoming the Spring. Sentiment about birds disappeared with Georgian Verse; and a modern ornithologist bids us regard the blackbird, thrush or nightingale as a mere torrid little bundle of conditioned reflexes, its song the automatic defiance of an aggressive property-owner, its nesting instinct dictated by the desire to cool a hot and itching bosom, which can only be soothed against the surface of an egg-shell. Yet these geese in their fountain-prison seemed to embody a positive purposeful enjoyment, as they dived vertically into the grey-green flood and streaked along the floor of the pool, to re-emerge delightedly clapping their wings, ruffling, preening, plume-caressing, with big moonstones of water still scattered on their backs and shoulders.

From a seat at the edge of the fountain, besides admiring the geese, I could also survey nearly the whole extent of the Great Harbour, which swings round through a curve of several miles and leaves a narrow entrance between Ortygia and the mainland. If Thucydides wrote his history in the classic form of a tragedy, where insolent pride leads to infatuation, and infatuation to eventual ruin, here is the theatre that saw the beginning of the

17

last act. Fifteen years had passed since Pericles delivered his famous Funeral Oration, praising the integrity and civilised restraint of the Athenian character, when the imperialist democracy, now grown rich and arrogant, equipped a formidable armada to extort the spoils of Sicily. "Never had a greater expedition been sent to a foreign land; never was there an enterprise in which the hope of future success seemed to be better justified by actual power."* Every ship was a separate masterpiece; for "everyone strove . . . that his own ship might excel both in beauty and in swiftness". The splendid freebooters, whose piratical foray was justified by the flimsiest of pretexts, received, before they left the Piraeus, a resounding civic farewell. Multitudes had assembled to watch them go; prayers were chanted in unison; and on each deck libations were poured from gold and silver chalices. At length the paean was raised, and the fleet put out to sea, at first in orderly procession, then the ships light-heartedly racing one another as far as the island of Aegina, whence they "hastened onwards to Corcyra, where the allies who formed the rest of the army were assembling . . ."

A century—half a century—ago, to remind an educated reader of the catastrophe described in the Seventh Book of Thucydides might have appeared a grave impertinence; and even today, during the present twilight of classical education, he may recollect the main outlines of that appalling drama: how the Athenians and their allies besieged but failed to conquer Syracuse, partly through over-optimism, partly through poor leadership—two of the original commanders were professional politicians—partly through some weakness of a rather more mysterious kind. Twice at least the Athenian forces were seized with sudden panic. Syracuse was to have been cut off by capturing and fortifying the high ground immediately behind it. This the Athenian

* Jowett's translation, here and elsewhere.

infantry were unable to do—at the climax of a night-engagement, for no reason that could afterwards be explained, they incontinently broke and ran; but the harbour was still full of their ships, and a way of escape and withdrawal still lay open to them. An eclipse of the moon, however, delayed their retreat; and, as the Athenian spirit declined, the Syracusans gathered confidence. Having checked their opponents at sea—for in the restricted spaces of the harbour their craft were more easily manoeuvrable than the heavier Athenian triremes, which were accustomed to frontal attacks, but found themselves at a disadvantage when exposed to lateral onslaughts—they proceeded to construct a boom across the narrow entrance-passage, and, disposing their warships, some in front of the boom, some to the left and right, waited until the besieged fleet should attempt a desperate breakthrough.

The Athenians were guilty men, confused by their sense of guilt like any tragic hero—that is the implication of Thucydides' narrative, though he nowhere overstresses it. They were bewildered by the resistance they met and the reverses that they suffered; for "the Sicilian were the only cities which they had ever encountered similar in character to their own, having the same democratic institutions and strong in ships, cavalry, and population. They were not able, by holding out the prospect of a change of government, to introduce an element of discord . . ." But guilt and despair are potent incentives to action; and in their preparations for escape the entrapped Athenians revealed all their natural energy, equipping the sides of their ships with grappling-irons—so that a vessel which charged them laterally should not slide away again—and embarking a large number of archers and javelin-throwers, since they were intended, as their commanders had told the troops, to "fight a land-battle on ship-board". The triremes with which the Athenians attacked—what was left of an armada of slightly over two hundred—were the remote and impressive ancestors of the present Mediterranean fishing-boats which lie rocking along the quay-side beneath the walls of Syracuse. Painted a lively blue or green, they bear on each side of the prow a boldly-stylised human eye; their sterns are sharp; and of the armoured rams with which their ancient prototypes breached and sank their adversaries, they still retain some reminiscence in the shape of a rudimentary beak. Sweeping eastwards against the boom, the assembled mass of the Athenian fleet must have been formidable. It brushed away its immediate opponents; it reached its first objective. But the boom would not immediately yield; and, while the Athenian crews were still struggling to unfasten the chains with which a long line of war-vessels, merchant-ships and small craft was securely lashed together, the bulk of the Syracusan forces came racing down on either wing; and the conflict, growing general, surged backward from the harbour-mouth.

Soon the whole harbour was crowded with manoeuvring and contending ships. "No previous engagement (declares Thucydides) had been so fierce and obstinate . . . Never did so many fight in so small a space . . ." But, unlike a modern historian, he omits to inform us either of the hour at which the engagement was joined or of the duration of the battle. Nor does he, as a contemporary writer would surely have done, though not it may be with the best results, attempt to convey the colour and light of the encircling landscape—the sun-dazzle glittering from shore to shore, the dark-blue expanse of the harbour torn by rhythmic oar-blades. Instead he concentrates on the dramatic essentials of a human tragedy, and relates how, as warship shuddered against warship, with splintering of oars and crash of broken timbers, the labouring crews became dazed and bewildered, and the shouting boatswains could not make their orders heard. From the harbour arose a prodigious hubbub—imagine, in addition to the mechanical din, several thousand bellicose, distracted, panic-stricken or agonizing Southerners simultaneously but discordantly giving voice to their excitement! And, along the shores, from the walls of Syracuse, and from the sloping ground beyond the walls of the city, where the Athenian forces were assembled as on the shallow tiers of seats that surround a Greek theatre, reverberated a continuous blast of triumph, rage and misery, which waxed and waned according both to the sympathies of the audience and the positions that they occupied. Spectators and actors were equally wide-spread; and, while some of the Athenians, witnessing the victory of their own ships, would frenziedly cheer them on and implore the gods they worshipped "not to take from them their hope of deliverance", others, seeing an Athenian reverse, "cried and shrieked aloud, and were by the sight alone more utterly unnerved than the defeated combatants themselves", and still others, as their fortunes wavered, "kept swaying their bodies to and fro in an agony of hope and fear . . . for at every instant they were all but saved and all but lost," adding to the immense cacophony of various sounds "wrung from a great host in extremity of danger".

At length the Syracusans began to prevail; the Athenian fleet in confusion rushed back toward its land-base, and the crews, leaping ashore, deserted their ships and fled helter-skelter into the fortified encampment. Then the army, "no longer divided in feeling", uttered "one universal groan of intolerable anguish" and hurried to guard the empty vessels or to man the walls and breastworks. But it was too late; and, although that evening Nikias pointed out that the Athenian fleet had still a numerical advantage, since it consisted of sixty ships, whereas the Syracusans now had less than fifty, the demoralised sailors refused to embark, and the Athenians determined to escape by retreating overland. The retreat from Moscow, though enacted on a far more extensive scale, can scarcely have been more horrifying. The beaten army was gradually cut to pieces; Nikias, a good man and a conscientious commander, with his colleague Demosthenes, was summarily put to death; and the survivors, seven thousand of them, were condemned to starve and rot in the Syracusan quarries, deep-dug concentration-camps enclosed by beetling rock walls. Here, says Thucydides, they sweltered under the midday sun, but shivered during autumn nights. "Being cramped for room they had to do everything on the same spot. The corpses of those who died from their wounds, exposure to heat and cold, and the like, lay heaped one upon another . . . Nothing was saved, and of the many who went forth few returned home. Thus ended the Sicilian expedition."

On coins minted after the Athenian collapse, Victory hovering with a wreath above the customary four-horse chariot—thin-legged horses nervously stamping and pawing, while the charioteer tightens the reins as he leans alertly forward—had for the citizens of Syracuse an especial patriotic value. But their liberties, saved in 415 B.C., had been lost before the end of the century, when, the Carthaginians becoming again aggressive, Dionysius, a gifted opportunist, half persuaded, half coerced them into totalitarian servitude. The dictator's rise followed a familiar pattern. Profiting by a national emergency, and by the fact that he alone seemed capable of dealing with it, Dionysius obtained extraordinary powers, alleged that his life was threatened and petitioned for a body-guard, used his body-guard as a private militia, and presently established an unlimited kingship. Yet there is no doubt that the Syracusan dictator possessed distinguished qualities. Dionysius today would, I suppose, have been called a technocrat; for his genius was managerial; and, whereas other and more ingenuous leaders depended upon the favour of the gods, the luck of the game, or treachery or physical courage, he would seem to have relied on his superior gifts of organisation and on the cleverness, co-ordinated by himself, of the artificers he had collected. He was a militarist who never fought if he could win a diplomatic victory, a power-politician, who did not refrain from violence, but was always glad to enact the rôle of the unassuming plain man. His technical achievements were indeed astonishing; and in the construction of new fortifications, new naval vessels and new engines of war he showed the ingenuity of a Leonardo. Syracuse during his reign, which lasted from 405 to 367 B.C., became a huge and crowded workshop. In the Great Harbour, lined with busy dockyards, were moored warships that had five banks of oars instead of the traditional three; while two hundred new ships were built, and a hundred and fifty reconditioned and refitted. In his arsenals, immense military machines, hitherto unknown to Sicily, reared their sharp-beaked silhouettes, engines many-armed as Briareus, which projected gigantic masses of rock and had a range of several hundred yards. "He prepared likewise (writes Diodorus Siculus) engines of battery of all fashions; and, that nothing might lack to render his assembled armaments magnificent and glorious, for further state and grace to the preparations he made a hundred and fifty thousand bucklers, or targets, as many swords and helmets, and caused to be forged fourteen thousand corselets, of all sorts of excellent workmanship; these he appointed and ordered to the horse, and to the colonels and captains of the foot, and to the mercenaries who were of his life-guard."

Native talent and valour were not neglected; but to the population of Syracuse Dionysius added a horde of foreign workmen and technicians, whom he organised and directed under Syracusan overseers. There were foreign artisans wherever one looked; "for, not only the porches and back-parts of the temples, but the public schools and walks, and galleries about the forum, and every place up and down were full of workmen'', drawn from the islands and mainland of Greece and the cities of southern Italy. The forests of Etna were ravaged to build his fleet; but his greatest and most enduring project was the fortress of Euryalus, the key-point of his system of defences, since it closed and dominated the whole of the plateau behind Syracuse. During their siege the Athenian forces had temporarily occupied this high ground; and such an advantage, Dionysius determined, should never again be within the grasp of an invading foreign army. Some three or four miles beyond the outskirts of the present suburbs, the plateau grows narrow and the ground tilts sharply downhill. Here Dionysius spanned the ridge with a colossal fortress, a wedge-shaped construction like a warship's beaked prow, from which walls ran backwards and outwards, embracing the whole upland and meeting the earlier walls of Syracuse on its northern and southern verges. One need not be a student of military architecture to find the ruins of Euryalus supremely odd and fascinating—the broad galleries and spacious stairways tunnelled through the limestone, the profound fosses and moats also cut in solid rock, the underground storerooms and magazines, and the wreckage of immense bastions, built of brobdingnagian cubes of beautifully-jointed but unmortared masonry. Into his masterpiece Dionysius seems to have flung the whole strength of his genius—a genius which, although as severely practical as that of Leonardo, in common with Leonardo's had also something strange about it. His, too, we feel, was a fantastic and romantic spirit which mere material achievement did not altogether satisfy. Yet the business of actual construction evidently delighted him; and Diodorus Siculus (a dull historian, who is always at his liveliest when he is writing of the Sicilian tyrant) describes Dionysius personally encouraging his engineers and craftsmen, taking his share of the work, "speaking kindly and courteously" to any man who did his job well, dispensing magnificent rewards and issuing invitations to banquets at his palace on Ortygia. Sixty-thousand freemen, besides an army of slaves and many thousand yokes of oxen bringing stones up from the quarries, are reputed to have raised the three northern miles of wall in slightly under three weeks. It was his aim, probably realised, to become the master of the most considerable and most strongly walled metropolis in any European country.

Hugely and rapidly though Syracuse spread, the entire space enclosed by Dionysius can never have been built over; but the modern city would rank as a small provincial town beside its ancient counterpart. On the tip of the ridge, beyond Euryalus, a rather woebegone village is packed around a signal-tower; but eastwards, behind the fortifications, there is no trace of modern building. One is alone in a sunny and windy void; the grass on the platforms and in the moats of the castle is full of miniature wild flowers; and, where the great grey blocks of Dionysius' wall have tumbled down the hill below, big round clumps of succulent spurge, bearing a thick crop of greenish-yellow blossoms, are dotted in a pleasingly conventional design among the ash-pale masonry. Returning to Syracuse, one passes the site of Tycha and Achradina, districts that many years before Dionysius' town-planning were already large and populous. Today they have completely disappeared. Immediately above the modern town, with its noisy shabby suburbs, the country unfolds as a gigantic lunar graveyard, a vast plateau of pallid calcareous rock, picked and scrubbed clean of any trace of antique splendour. "Unspeakable desolation", wrote Gregorovius, an itinerant German scholar who visited Syracuse at a time when Sicily was still a Bourbon province: "interminable stony plains, or wild labyrinths, traversed by hermit-like capuchins". Nor has a scattering of small

new houses greatly changed the prospect. The stone benches of
the Greek theatre look out over the harbour across the sidings
of a railway-station; but from the topmost circle a crooked lane,
cut ten or twelve feet deep, leads upwards between rock walls,
with huge funereal pigeon-holes, the violated tombs of rich
Syracusan citizens, hollowed out on either hand, dark, dusty,
forbidding, irregularly-shaped crevices, some of them small and
narrow, others lofty and wide enough to receive a numerous
family, but all vacant, smelling of mould and damp, all seeming
to exhale a sour breath of loneliness. Underfoot the natural rock
pavement is deeply scored and rutted. Here are the wheel-marks
of waggons and chariots; but, as Gregorovius perplexedly noticed,
these tracks (which must have taken many years to develop,
"since the limestone of Syracuse does not take the impress of
wheels so easily as the Roman tufa") rarely follow a parallel
course and, like lines on the palm of the hand, diverge, converge
and intersect. Similar tracks, similarly erratic, appear beside the
adjacent quarries. Indeed the whole landscape possesses the same
disturbing and enigmatic character. Almost everything that
human ingenuity can do to stone has been laboriously done to it;
immense catacombs have been excavated, which stretch beneath
the hill in "endless streets and lanes, chambers, niches, squares
and halls": innumerable rock-tombs have been cut, and stupendous quarries carved out: while the entire surface of the plateau
is pitted and creased and corrugated with cisterns and shallow
vacant sepulchres, with the vestiges of walls and the foundations
of vanished houses—remains of the imposing city enlarged by
Dionysius.

Little loose stone remains. No less remarkable than the
evidence of human attacks upon the landscape's rocky structure
is the complete disappearance of the buildings with which the
plateau was once burdened. What can have happened to such a

weight of masonry? Generation after patient generation may have
uprooted it and carried it away to form the material of its own
buildings; but Ortygia, towards which the city receded, is not a
very large island and, since the creation of the original settlement,
was always densely built-up. Greater Syracuse, as if under the
influence of some maleficent incantation, has utterly demateria-
lised, leaving behind it on the heights only a wind-swept lunar
emptiness. We might assume that historians who wrote of its
extent and majesty were imaginative panegyrists, could we not
examine the quarries from which the stone was hacked out. In a
learned divagation on Piranesi's *Prisons*, Aldous Huxley has remarked that their most disquieting feature is "the perfect
pointlessness" that characterises every composition; ". . . the
staircases lead nowhere, the vaults support nothing . . . Below
stand great machines incapable of doing anything in particular
. . ." The quarries of Syracuse were by no means pointless since,
besides furnishing stone, they served again and again as places of
imprisonment; yet they have something of the nightmare quality,
the chilly subaqueous gloom, the air of fantastic inconsequence
we find in Piranesi's etchings. All are over a hundred feet deep,
some considerably deeper; and everywhere the strange shapes
imposed upon the swelling and impending rock-faces seem to
have had an imaginative rather than a utilitarian origin; as if an
inspired but diabolical artist had set out to build a dungeon that
should not only contain the prisoner's body but should also entrap
and gradually undermine his spirit, intensifying his despair to the
pitch of distraction by the peculiarity of the forms that day and
night surrounded him.

Thus, rising from the levelled floor, stand oddly-twisted sen-
tinel-pillars, isolated for no ascertainable reason, on which we
expect to see either some stylite-victim doomed to solitary con-
finement, or perhaps an armed guard, hoisted there by ropes and

pulleys, brooding over the aimless malefactors who drift around the column's base. The details of these extraordinary excavations, like the details of Piranesi's underground gaols, are bewilderingly elaborate: they too are a world in themselves, with ascents and descents and dark forbidding crevices, a world from which normality has been banished and hope has been excluded. Into the foot of a cliff, for example, masons have cut a spacious, low-roofed, irregularly-shaped gallery, large enough to take an encampment of several dozen people; and the family of rope-makers who work there today, because the perpetually dripping cavern gives them the room they need for the operation of their rope-walk, have a look in the half-light of pallid dwarfish troglodytes. But the chief oddity of the quarries is, of course, the seventy-foot high aperture to which some early tourist (who may or may not have been the painter Caravaggio) gave the romantic title of "The Ear of Dionysius". The tyrant, it was generally believed, sat above in a concealed niche, listening to the echoed conversations of his political captives. Certainly the narrow S-shaped opening, which is nowhere wider than thirty-six feet and has a depth of some two hundred, will produce, when invoked, an immense booming stuttering echo; but in the rumble it punctually returns—hoarse and resonantly inhuman as the roar of rutting elk or sea-lion—no separate sentences or words can be distinguished. That the cave is a natural freak was suggested not long ago by a sceptical English traveller; but he omitted to note that on the whole surface of the smoothly narrowing, sinuously closing passage, which winds into the rock just as the convolutions of the ear wind into the cranium, there are tens of thousands of delicate chisel-marks, unpleasantly suggestive of the pores of human skin. Yes, the "Ear" was evidently man-made. But why it should have been planned and executed remains a formidable problem—a problem, however, that gradually dropped behind

me, as I walked home through the rich cool-smelling garden
which at present fills the quarry-depths. Among dark-green
orchard foliage hung enormous moon-pale lemons; mats of red-
fruited prickly-pear spilt over the edge of the cliffs; and between
the rock walls the whistling song of a few bold southern birds had
a peculiar flute-like clarity.

II

Rᴏᴜɴᴅ ᴀ ʙᴇɴᴅ of the broad dusty road that
winds down from the hill city of Agrigento towards its ruined
temples, a mule was shying and rearing, terrified by the racket
of an ascending motor-bus. At its head was a boy of seven or
eight; the mule's plunges had wrenched his arm—it was a strong
and youngish animal—and swinging the slack of the halter rope
he began to lash it frantically. It balked, stubborn and stiff-
legged, then broke into a trot and tried to drag him downhill.
Dangling furiously from the halter, he forced it to a walking pace.
Again it refused to budge, again it attempted to bolt; while the
boy, cursing it in a shrill voice, hoarse with fear and anger,
frightened himself but above all enraged by the rebellious conduct of this sweating, trembling and side-swerving piece of un-
wieldy animal mechanism, aimed savage kicks at its legs and
presently, as high as his foot could reach, at the barrel-shaped
ribs and belly. Should a traveller interfere? With verbal remon-
strances in bad Italian to a boy who spoke Sicilian dialect? By a
display of superior strength and skill, which would probably have
ended in humiliating failure? By a gift of money which would
have caused him to be regarded as mad, or as the prospective

purchaser of a mule which he would have been obliged to turn loose or consign to a similar existence with another peasant family? So, self-reproachful and undecided, he left them at the bend of the road—an emblematic group representing Fear and Cruelty, demons that, however deliberately we reject their influence, however plausibly we may trace them back to their ultimate social origin, still arouse a disturbing, not unresponsive vibration somewhere in the human consciousness. We are seldom as far from them as we hope and pretend; and, confronted with the spectacle of violence and terror, we feel that we are entering the presence of an older range of deities, whose effect on our imaginations, sufficiently familiar in childhood, has never quite been shaken off.

In every religious system of the ancient world, the dark gods occupied a considerable niche; and, whereas classicists of the nineteenth century showed us Olympus as a kind of heavenly Parthenon, white, gleaming, immaculate, peopled by a divine race of human appearance but more than human comeliness, modern scholars have. exploded that view of the Olympian hierarchy, pointing to numerous relics of gloomier cults and ages—venerated lumps of wood and stone, primitive sanguinary gods and their animal-headed consorts. Religions and civilisations differ in the extent to which the divinities of the spiritual under-world—or, as a contemporary psychologist might prefer to say, of the unexplored subconscious—are recognised or disregarded. No one, for instance, who has entered Peking's Lama Temple, where the atmosphere of terror and mystery is heightened by the solemn minotaur-bellowing of twelve-foot brazen horns, or has climbed to the gaudy pavilion perched upon a wooded hillock from which a many-headed, many-armed monster glares down across the Forbidden City, will have forgotten how completely the Tantric or Thibetan rite—the debased off-shoot of the

Buddhist faith that found official favour with the latest Chinese
Emperors—overlaid and obliterated its earlier, gentler aspects.
In place of a philosophic nihilism we encounter the wildest
forms of unabashed diabolism. The radiant yet pensive saints of
classical Chinese art, their eyelids weighted with infinite com-
passion, resignation in each fluid line of their supply-folded bodies,
have been ousted by rank behind rank of raging northern devils,
who sup blood from half an inverted skull, flourish an immense
battery of threatening, clawing pseudopods, and even in the
ecstasy of love, when a female demon, her tongue extruded,
rushes to impale herself on her grimacing counterpart, remain as
mindlessly inimical to humanity as the Pacific typhoon or the
Himalayan snow-storm. Here is, if not the ultimate degradation,
at least a grotesque distortion of the religious impulse, man's
final act of surrender before the demons that surround him.
Some cults—indeed the majority—have had both a dark and a
light side; but there have also been phases of civilisation from
which, though rarely for very long, the dark divinities have been
thrust out. The ancient dragon has been cast into the pit, the
mouth of Hades walled over.

Temporarily in the *douceur de vivre* it has proved possible to
forget the fears and pains of living; and such a moment would
appear to have been enjoyed by the prosperous citizens of
Akragas, the city which in Roman times was known as Agri-
gentum, which the Italians called Girgenti and which, during
Mussolini's rule, they re-named Agrigento. Of Syracuse Cicero
wrote that so sober were its inhabitants, so practical and hard-
working, that they bore little resemblance to other Greeks,
whose effeminate and volatile temperament disconcerted and disgusted stolid Roman businessmen. While Syracuse was the home
of skill and knowledge, a background for the speculations of
Plato and the discoveries of Archimedes, Akragas was the city of

5   *TRAPANI: A house in the ancient ghetto*

6 *ENNA: Chiesa del Carmine*

7 *ERYX, above Trapani*

pleasure, peopled by men and women less concerned with the
arduous search for first causes than with gliding smoothly and
pleasantly across the surface of existence, admiring the exquisite
bloom a well-tended surface offers. Sensible hedonists, reasonable
voluptuaries, like Homer's Phaeacians they were neither athletes
nor adventurers but, as Alkinous suavely explained to his guest
when he described his happy subjects, "ever delighted in feasts
and dances and music, in frequent changes of clothing and hot
baths and love and sleep". They were proud, too, of the city
they owned, the long line of temples looking out over the African
Sea, the splendour of their private dwellings, even the beauty of
their funerary monuments, some (writes Diodorus Siculus)
"adorned with the charging horses of the heroes there interred,
others with those little birds that the children, both girls and
boys, fed and bred up in their parents' houses". To provide fish
at public banquets, they had constructed a huge stew-pond just
beyond the city walls, haunted by swans and many-coloured
water-fowl; and, as for the personal state they kept, "their nice
and delicate way of living, (till it came to their very children) . . .
was to that degree, that they wore garments of cloth of gold,
and had their water-pots, and boxes of ointment, of gold and
silver". Their hospitality was renowned, perhaps a trifle osten-
tatious; and Polyclitus the historian, according to Diodorus,
speaks of having inspected a celebrated wine-cellar, "in which
were contained three hundred great vessels, cut out of one and
the same rock, each of which received an hundred hogsheads",
and "a cistern of pure white tempered mortar, containing a
thousand hogsheads, out of which the liquor ran into the vessels".

With nearly a quarter of a million inhabitants, of whom only
one in ten, however, was a fully enfranchised citizen, Akragas
was designated by Pindar "the loveliest city of mortals", the
"eye of Sicily", "the sacred settlement beside the river", a

33

c

"lofty city lavish above all in gifts to the gods".* More sharply Plato, that inveterate foe to easy satisfaction, observed that the men of Akragas built as if they had no thought of death, and dined as if the hour of the dinner-party was expected to be their last one. Possibly they were right to do so; for these opulent and pleasure-loving burgesses who had "grown very rich by their trading with the Libyans" and sold the produce of their olive-yards in Carthaginian markets, as inescapably as modern Europeans lived beneath a constant shadow. Since the beginning of the fifth century, Carthaginian armies had been encamped on the Sicilian coast-line, spear-head of the warrior-trader race which, except for a few noble coins, evidently designed by captive Greek artificers, has left behind no art, no literature, nothing visible, palpable, audible to redeem and recommend it. Carthage is a gap in history; and out of the void reverberate the names of its generals, sonorous and metallic—Hannibal, Hamilcar, Hasdrubal, soldiers of a commercial empire, cruel and efficient barbarians perpetually at war with beauty, peace and happiness. Often defeated, they often returned; and in the year 406 B.C. Himilco and Hannibal son of Gisco planned to capture Akragas. The citizens, though they had little real appetite for conflict, managed to put up a brave face. They made preparations to resist a blockade, hired a Spartan general, and appealed for assistance to their Syracusan allies. The barbarians landed, and they consented to man the walls; but the habits of freedom and independence were difficult to throw off; and "at the very height of the siege . . . a decree was made, that none of them that were upon guard in the night, should have above a bed, a tent, a woollen mantle, and two pillows . . . This seemed a hard law", a grievous "disturbance

* For a full account of ancient Akragas, see Kathleen Freeman: *Greek City States*. Though renowned for its luxurious worldliness, Akragas, it is proper to add, was an important centre of the mystery-religion of Demeter and Persephone.

to their ease and repose", by which we may judge (Diodorus remarks) "how soft and luxurious they were in all other things". Nevertheless they might have prevailed, had their allies not abandoned them; and it was only when food ran short that the Akragantines decided they must leave their city. Some committed suicide rather than lose their possessions—those in whom the love of life had become completely identified with the protective material envelope they had built around their inner selves; but an immense disorganised convoy took the road for the friendly city of Gela,* "so that all the ways and country towards Gela swarmed with a promiscuous multitude of women and children; amongst whom were young ladies, who though they had now changed their former soft and delicate way of living, into the fatigues and sorrows of tedious journeys, yet being quickened and stirred up by fear, bore all difficulties with eminent patience". Looking back to the city they adored, some of them may have caught sight of a tremendous conflagration, illuminating the row of temples built upon its seaward edge. A certain Gellias, "eminent above the rest of his countrymen in the greatness of his wealth, and integrity of his conversation", had sought refuge in the temple of Athene, hoping that the Carthaginians might respect the shrines of the gods. Disappointed, he set fire to the building and perished in the destruction of its vast accumulated treasure.

A cautionary tale for the epicurean; but the deliberate cultivation of the *douceur de vivre* has other disadvantages. Since contentment is probably an unnatural condition, epicureans are apt to develop a curious strain of pettiness: the works they produce have none of the grandeur sometimes achieved by more passionate and more deeply troubled artists. Thus it is the placing of Akragas' ruined temples, high on a long ridge between the

* It was from Gela, founded by settlers from Rhodes and Crete, that the city of Akragas had originally been colonised.

sea-shore and the modern town, rather than the quality of their architecture, that gives them their distinction. The Temple of Concord, for example, labelled by guide books "one of the best-preserved ancient temples in existence", reminded me of Byron's remark when, accompanied by a Cambridge friend, he first set eyes upon the Parthenon and observed with a provocative sneer that he found it "very like the Mansion House". For the Temple of Concord is unmistakably a tidy civic edifice, neat and compact and harmoniously regular. But the glistening white marble-hard stucco with which the temples were sheathed has little by little flaked off, exposing the warm surface of the yellow porous lime-stone; and from the shrine of Hera at the end of the ridge the sacred rock falls gradually away towards the gigantic remains of the Temple of Olympian Zeus in an intricate, endlessly delightful pattern of yellow, green and silver drab—the silver of olives, the dark green of orange groves and the lighter, livelier green of peach trees, broken by the tawny colour of standing columns and rock and tumbled masonry, among fountains of vaporous fruit-blossom that last into the late spring.

The Greeks chose the sites of their cities and sanctuaries not merely for practical but also for religious—or, which perhaps comes almost to the same thing, for psychological and aesthetic —reasons. The temples of Akragas, Selinus and Segesta are not only boldly and beautifully placed, but they occupy situations in which the whole mood of the landscape—difficult to describe but, when it is unfriendly, impossible to escape from—seems especially harmonious. A friend subject to recurrent attacks of gloom once declared that he could cover the entire map of Europe pointing out the "*cafard-centres*". Santorin I remember, was a particularly dangerous island; but there were other plague-spots in which all the nervous apprehensions and grim recollec-tions of the human race appeared to have been concentrated.

Similarly, there are corners of the earth where the human burden
loses its weight, the body fits the spirit as a glove the hand inside
it, where every movement and nearly every word promises,
momentarily at least, to acquire the same coherence. I had felt
calm and secure among the ruins of Agrigento, seated on the
steps of Hera's temple, picking and trying to draw some of the
wild flowers in the grass around—tall, angular, spiky asphodel,
bright yellow snapdragon, minute cardinal-red sweet peas—and,
two days later, the same sensation returned at Selinus or Selinunte, a wide table-land broken off above the sea in an abrupt
and rocky cliff edge. The sea itself here is peculiarly well-
mannered, neither listless as in some parts of the Mediterranean,
which have barely determination to push ashore their own refuse
but keep apathetically turning and mumbling a fringe of ancient
sea-rubbish, nor truculent and boisterous like Atlantic breakers.
Curling waves pawed at the dark volcanic sand masterfully yet
cheerfully; the beach was spacious and clean, hard enough underfoot to make for pleasant walking. Inland, behind and around the
temples, stretched during the spring months acres of green wheat
and deliciously-scented flowering beans; and distant farmhouses
stood out in light-toned cubes of masonry, giving just that re-
minder of human existence which, as Poussin and Claude
discovered, the perfect classical landscape needs. For a time we
were quite alone; but a young goat-herd presently emerged from
among the mountainous ruins, driving his flock towards the edge
of the cliff, through labyrinths of stone and in and out of the
bushes of spurge and wild rosemary. To watch goats feeding is
usually enjoyable; for they have none of the mechanical assiduity
of browsing sheep or oxen, but trickle and spill in a river of
animation across the ground they pasture on, hooves clicking and
scrabbling against stones and potsherds, mounting a huge block
in a single sudden leap, with a dip of the horns and a shake of the

37

beard as lightly leaping out of view, every goat pursuing a separate course, drifting, side-stepping and prancing apart, yet, while bells tinkle and the goat-herd whistles and shouts, always slowly reassembling. Moreover the goat is one of the very few animals which give the impression that they see human beings clearly. Now and then it will pause in its meal, a tuft of green-stuff in the corner of its mouth, and turn on the stranger a look, not of fear or respect, but of cold and glassy interest—a devilish glance, with its twisted horns, its long narrow priapic mask and the beard which is formidable but somehow never venerable.

Besides the goat-herd and the custodian of the ruins, a small, friendly, inconspicuous man who bore the splendid name of Barbarossa, we met, strolling through the fields, the local *carabiniere*, with a round youthful face beneath his patent-leather hat, who told us he came from the mainland, since to put a Sicilian policeman among Sicilians was always inadvisable, and talked at length about Giuliano, the celebrated bandit chief of Monte Lepre. Rather surprisingly for a representative of the law, he admitted that he was on Giuliano's side; the bandit, he said, was a *buono ragazzo*; and almost every crime committed within a hundred miles of his native mountain was written off, in nine instances out of ten altogether unjustifiably, as Giuliano's doing. Later we were overtaken on the shore by a crafty dark-browed peasant. Cautiously in the hollow of his hand he showed us some fragments of bronze that he professed to have dug up—a delicate ancient fish-hook and a few battered coins, displaying on one side the head of a tutelary nymph, on the other a long-legged horse accompanied by a palm-tree. He drove a hard bargain, to which I presently agreed—not, however, because I much admired the coins but because I wished to carry off some solid memorial of Selinunte, of its rippling verdant landscape and the strong scent of the flowering beans, the bloom of light that lay upon fields and waves, and the mysterious impression of calm and well-being that seemed to descend from the air or rise from the earth like dew, but was destined gradually to disappear once we had taken the road again . . .

A second glance at the coins I had bought assured me they were valueless. Moreover they were probably late. For weren't the horse and the palm-tree Carthaginian emblems, and didn't this mean that they belonged to a period after the Carthaginian conquest? Selinus, too, collapsed in the wave of aggression which, at the end of the fifth and the beginning of the fourth centuries, overwhelmed Akragas, Gela, Himera, Kamerina and gravely threatened Syracuse. As the westernmost of Grecian cities, Selinus had pursued a pacific policy towards its barbarian neighbours: the Selinuntines had even sided with the Carthaginians against Akragas and Syracuse: but their collaboration was of no help to them in 409 B.C., when Hannibal invested the city, breached the walls after a fiercely contested siege and, step by step, fought his way into the central market-place. There followed a particularly hideous sack, with universal rape and slaughter, the barbarians raging through the streets carrying bandoliers of severed hands or "the heads of the slain upon the points of their swords and spears". Yet, although the Carthaginians exceeded "all other men in impiety", they would not, or could not, destroy the Selinuntine sacred edifices, which continued to stand until, some time during the Dark Ages, they were demolished by an earthquake. This prodigious catastrophe, which almost completely overthrew seven unusually large and massively-constructed temples, occurred during a period when history was no longer written, or when, by men capable of writing, the western end of Sicily was very rarely visited. But a number of admirable metopes—the square panels of bas-relief placed at intervals beneath the frieze of every Doric building—have been removed to the protection of the museum at Palermo. They range from *Europa on the Bull* and *Perseus beheading the Gorgon*, carved at the beginning of the sixth century, to the splendid *Herakles subduing an Amazon* and *Zeus welcoming Hera*, created in the early fifth. Only a hundred years divide them—but what a gulf of feeling! Perseus still lives in the archaic world of fairy-tales. His divine protectress smiling behind him, smiling himself broadly and self-confidently, he seizes the Gorgonian top-knot while he slips the blade of his sword underneath the monster's chin. But Herakles and Zeus have entered the world of adult emotion and adult understanding. The irresistible strength of the hero is in poignant and dramatic contrast to the comparative weakness of the Amazon who, her foot pinned below his, reels away from the final blow he is just about to deal her; and Zeus and Hera—an extraordinarily ingenious piece of formal composition, beautifully designed to fill up the space dictated by the architect—produce an impression of emotional, even erotic, intensity seldom met in Greek sculpture, as the god, who is half reclining, his hand grasping her upraised wrist, draws towards his embrace the reluctant virginal goddess. The backgrounds of such reliefs, probably the figures too, were always brightly coloured. So were the triglyphs—the geometrical plaques arranged between the metopes —parts of the glistening white columns, the cornices and pediments. The effect of an Hellenic temple, surrounded by a grove of tripods, altars, votive statues, must have been as exuberantly polychromatic as that of any thirteenth-century Gothic church.

Taking the southward road from Syracuse, and after the incomparable city of Noto (which I must attempt to describe elsewhere) turning west and north-west, the clockwise perambulator of Sicily presently arrives at its extreme western angle, at Marsala, a pleasant but prosy town, dedicated to the wine-trade, and Trapani, the ancient Drepana, a noisy modern sea-port

beneath the rampart of Mount Eryx. Here and at Marsala, which
the Romans knew as Lilybaeum, were Carthaginian strong-
points; and on the summit of Mount Eryx, beside a temple to the
Carthaginian god Melkarth, was a famous shrine of Aphrodite,
identified with Astarte or Ashtaroth, the Phoenician moon-
goddess, served by "women sacred to the goddess"—in other
words, by temple prostitutes—whom "the inhabitants of Sicily"
and of neighbouring regions had "offered in accomplishment of
their vows". A legend of pleasure still clings to this forbidding
mountain-mass; and even today the women of Eryx, renamed
Monte San Giuliano, are celebrated, if not for their facility, at
least for their unusual beauty. Trapani, nevertheless, is not a place
to pause in; despite the existence of one or two exceedingly
sumptuous Baroque churches, their altars and side-chapels magnificently inlaid with many-coloured marbles, the impression it
makes on a traveller is neither cheerful nor hospitable. Such is
the effect in far-western Sicily of the Carthaginian heritage; the
human type is darker and surlier; the personality of towns and
villages seems to have undergone a subtle alteration. One is
conscious of the shadow of Africa, like the evening shadow of
some oppressive land-mark flung across a sun-lit prospect.

Moving towards Segesta we came in sight of Europe again.
There, seen through a nick in the skyline, was the Temple of
Demeter, small and far-off but beautifully distinct against a
neighbouring mountain-side. At a closer view, one notes that its
columns are completely spherical, built of circular drums unbroken by the customary Doric grooves. For the huge building
remained unfinished; its pillars were to have been ornamented
after they had been set up; but, owing to poverty or the constant
vicissitudes of Sicilian affairs, the work was never undertaken.
The ancient city, which climbed the opposite slope, has disappeared, leaving behind it only a thick scattering of broken tiles

41

and potsherds. The shrine of Demeter stands entirely alone, wrapped in such an atmosphere of romantic solitude as I have encountered nowhere else. If Selinunte is the most poetic of Sicilian temple sites and Agrigento the most urbane, Segesta is the loneliest. Not that it is difficult to reach or far from a highway; yet even the conscientious efforts of Mussolini's government, which since my last visit had driven a motor road to the foot of the hill, provided a wooden hut for the convenience of tourists, and begun to construct a kind of municipal rockery with cactus-spikes and hardy shrubs, have scarcely spoiled its isolation—the air of loneliness that weighs on the temple itself, an immense quadrangle of grey columns about the grassy unpaved sanctuary floor, or the penetrating emptiness and remoteness of the vast surrounding landscape.

Above and beyond the ruins, dominating but not dwarfing them, tower the limestone precipices of the range called Monte Barbaro. But there is a deep gorge between the temple and the mountain; and from its edge one looks down on a looped and tangled river, with clear pools lodged like fragments of green glass among the rocks and pebble banks. Somewhere a distant cascade kept up continuous water-music; and now and then, out of the walls of the ravine, blue rock doves would flash into the air and whirl off down the gulf below, their flight an explosion of sound and colour—very different from the flight of the jackdaws which wheeled and drifted round the temple-eaves, dusky and silent-winged but incessantly talkative, with metallic voices sadder and keener than those of any rookery. Green lizards basked on the steps and flickered away to the crevices of the porous limestone columns. Otherwise Segesta was lifeless; and when, at the bottom of the hill, a man in a peaked cap appeared and stood leaning on his bicycle, he seemed an emanation of the landscape he sprang from, barely capable of answering the simplest questions that we asked him. The theatre, he indicated, was somewhere above us, pointing vaguely to the opposite hillside and to a rough track which climbed and vanished across a rocky shoulder. We had a sultry and exhausting walk. Ancient Segesta must have been a hill-city, with streets as precipitous and twisted as those of Ragusa or Agrigento. Only broken pottery and tiles remain: shards of earthenware have a permanence denied to solid masonry. Then, just over the brow of the slope, we came on the grey wall buttressing the theatre circle; for, whereas most Greek theatres are hollowed from the native rock, this theatre has been artificially raised, to command the tremendous sweep of the valley that drops away in front of it, mile after cloud-fretted mile, rising at last to steep cultivated uplands and further ragged mountain ridges.

Here the wind blew through spurge and asphodel; and the air of loneliness that envelopes Segesta assumed a different quality. It was coloured by a sense of exaltation—the exaltation that comes of space and height, a mood to which both Greek and English romantic poets have proved particularly sensitive. One thinks of Prometheus, pinned to a Caucasian rock, surveying the "unnumbered laughter" of ocean far beneath him, and of Ion, in the temple courtyard, apostrophising "sun and light of day and the heavenly ripples of a flying cloud". Segesta, like every Greek theatre, arouses the poetic dramatist who may lie buried and forgotten somewhere even in the literary journalist. The spirit of the place urges creative expression. Some terrible figure should tread that stage: lines of memorable choric beauty should be chanted from the dancing floor. Evidently the actors must be larger than life; for realism would dwindle into insignificance against this prodigious prospect of sky and valley and mountain-slope; and, indeed, the Greek drama, so far as it has been preserved and we can profess to understand it, is probably closer to

43

the dramas of the East—for instance, to the Japanese *No* play—
than to the type of drama accepted in England since the
Restoration. The *No* actor does not walk: he glides across the
stage with phantom stealth and smoothness. From his mask
comes not the magnified and exaggerated voice of an ordinary
human being, but a sound as impressively remote from life as the
sighing of wind through trees, the groaning of a storm-vexed
branch or the crepitation of a distant avalanche. Sites chosen for
Greek theatres—in Taormina looking along an incomparably
beautiful coastline: in Syracuse commanding a nobly spacious
sea-inlet—require just that suggestion of extra-human majesty,
which was emphasised by the actor's mask, by his thick-soled
buskins and, no doubt, by the stylised gait and gestures with
which he made his entrance. Could such a drama be ever revived
—a drama including both the light and dark, Baudelaire's horror
of existence and his ''ecstasy of living''? Upon the empty stage,
beneath the noble curve of the shallow empty stone seats,
imagination began to sketch in scenes, evoking a portentous
personage, almost supplying the sonorous lines he uttered. *Almost*
—for between the verses one has nearly written, images that
perpetually hover a fraction out of arm's length, and the verses
captured and finally written down, stretches a gulf wide and deep
as one of the Syracusan quarries. Only genius could bridge the
chasm; and there was no genius to bring back to Segesta the
figures that should people it. So the appropriate drama remains
unwritten—another volume in that ghostly shelf where an author
preserves the masterpieces he has planned and knows that he
cannot hope to achieve, works more simple yet more profound,
more straightforward yet more allusive, more poetic yet more
firmly based upon direct experience, than any book of his con-
fection that will ever reach the publisher's hands.

III

Monte Lepre—the Legend of Giuliano—Mafia—A
Puppet Play—Peasant Life—the Citadel of Enna—
Demeter and Persephone—Flowers and Pastoral Poetry
—Theocritus at Alexandria

Approaching palermo, the coastal road
from the west runs beneath Monte Lepre. On stormy days when
its top is hidden by clouds, and curling vapours boil and fume
up its almost perpendicular gullies, "Hare Mountain" recalls
some tremendous Alpine fastness, evoked by the Byronic imagination of an early nineteenth-century steel-engraver. Bold and
craggy and forbidding enough, it had the added charm, when I
passed beneath it, of being the refuge and base of a renowned
Sicilian brigand. Giuliano was still a potent figure, making regular
appearances in the Sicilian press and enjoying the publicity
accorded him by journalists all over Europe. Female journalists
were particularly attentive; and, during our stay in Palermo, an
enterprising Scandinavian scribbler, known as "la Zilliacus,"
was arrested climbing the slopes of the mountain where she
claimed that she had already spent some days or weeks in her
bandit-lover's hiding-place. Taken to a police-station, she broke
a window, damaged furniture, insulted and assaulted the gendar-
merie and uttered terrible threats of Giuliano's vengeance. The
local papers, though at the time much preoccupied with the

apprehension of an especially ghoulish English criminal, *"il vampiro di Londra"*, canvassed the affair at length, paying particular attention to its amatory aspects, with an eloquence that must have delighted both Giuliano and his self-styled mistress. The bandit, indeed, was an exceedingly vain young man; and had it not been for his personal vanity, he might have escaped an early death.

Foreign commentators sometimes assumed that he was a member of the Mafia. In fact, nothing could have been more out of harmony with the practices of that ancient and respected institution than his showy exploits and vainglorious public statements. A small black-market operator who happened to kill a policeman, thereafter took to the hills and developed a large-scale business of brigandage and blackmail, he had little in common with the silent, discreet, sober, always unobtrusive, often elderly personages who control the Mafia throughout Sicily . . . But what *is* the Mafia? I began to enquire, tentatively at first, fearful I might be trespassing on an awkward or a forbidden subject. Sicilian acquaintances, however, showed not the least embarrassment, and answered my questions with alacrity, even with a touch of pride. For the Mafia has its roots in the past, not only in Sicilian history but in the native character, moulded by over two thousand years of alien domination. The island was always an occupied country—colonised by the Greeks who drove the indigenous Sikels into the rugged central districts: by the Carthaginians who harried the Greeks, and by the Romans who substituted their empire for the Carthaginian yoke, importing tax-gatherers and oppressive governors, of whom Verres, prosecuted by Cicero, was the notorious arch-type. Cicero's *Verrine Orations* give an extraordinary, though possibly exaggerated, picture of that voracious *parvenu*, travelling in state across his plundered province, never on horseback like a decent

Roman, but like a middle-eastern prince in a litter supported by eight servile bearers, reclining upon a "cushion of transparent Maltese embroidery stuffed with rose leaves, he himself wearing one garland on his head and another round his neck, and putting to his nostrils a gauze bag woven of the finest linen with delicate sprigs and a filling of rose petals". His requisitions devoured the harvests: his appetite for works of art, omnivorous and un-discriminating, violated the sanctity of many famous temples. Verres symbolised Republican Rome at its worst and stupidest; and after the Romans, besides a multitude of barbarian invaders, came Byzantine Greeks, Saracens, Normans, Spaniards and Italians of the mainland, each leaving behind a distinct trace— frequently a splendid and memorable trace—of the power they had exercised, none of them completely assimilated to the country they had held down.

Thus the established government was invariably suspect, identified in the Sicilian mind with some form of corruption or foreign exploitation. Judges and police were usually venal. The Mafia is a permanent Resistance Movement, a law beyond the law, operating at a level where legality is powerless. A word from the local Mafia-chief may bring a burglar hat in hand to his victim's doorstep, begging to be allowed to restore the stolen goods, apologising profusely for the preposterous mistake he made. The Mafia warns or punishes wrong-doers, settles disputes and also avenges the wounded honour of those who serve it faithfully; and a large landowner, who befriended us while we were in Palermo, told us that at that moment he was endeavouring, so far without success, to engineer a peace-treaty between a fellow landowner, who had offended or insulted a *Mafioso*, and the Mafia high command. As it was, the wretched offender could not go home to his country house. The Mafia did not threaten his life. They merely regretted that they could not guarantee his

47

safety. He might be shot down at any turn of the road; and, assuming that he remained unhurt, his servants would quietly leave him and provisions fail to reach him. He had offered to wipe out his offence with money, to pay whatever ransom they might care to name. The reply was a decided negative. Money lost its value, when Honour was in question.

A jealous regard for his personal honour, carried to chivalric lengths, is said always to have been characteristic of the Sicilian peasant's outlook. A wife's infidelity is punished by death: the innocence of an unmarried girl is rigorously supervised: and "I defy you to look at—what I call really *look at*—a woman any-where in the country" remarked an informant whose idea of "looking" was no doubt based on the customs of the mainland, where to examine every unknown female one passes with lingering sexual curiosity is the good-natured practice of most Italian town-dwellers. The Sicilians are still a romantic race, judging at least by popular preferences in the field of art and story-telling: scenes of the legends of Charlemagne and his knights cover the panels of the painted carts they ride in, and the Paladins interminably reappear among the characters of the puppet-plays. The puppet-drama continues to draw an enthusiastic audience. There is a well-known theatre in Palermo, another in Catania; but the second is hidden away in a somewhat wild and slummy neighbourhood; and, before he agreed to take us there, our guardian of the moment explained that negotiations would be necessary. Those negotiations were conducted at length; but after a series of mysterious telephone calls it was arranged that we should drive with our Catanian friend to one of the main thoroughfares and pick up an unknown guide who would conduct us to a meeting-place. The guide, when we had picked him up, was careful to observe the best traditions of conspiratorial literature. He would not name the piazza for which we were

48

8   NOTO: Chiesa di S. Domenico

9   PALERMO: Fountain in the Piazza Pretoria

10 *PLASTERWORK PANEL by Giacomo Serpotta*

11 *FORTITUDE by Giacomo Serpotta*

12 *DECORATIVE FIGURE by Giacomo Serpotta*

bound, but preferred to mutter quick directions as we drove along the evening streets. In a darkened alley we stopped at a door; he knocked for admittance, whispered to an old woman, vanished through a wicket-gate, re-emerged, instructed us to drive on and presently told us to dismount at a small and squalid café. Around the walls sat a collection of *figurants*, mute and watchful over their coffee-cups, perfect theatrical representations of a gangster's body-guard. Our host, on the other hand, the local *Capo di Mafia*, who had with him a Sicilian deputy to whom we had already been presented, wore the neat uniform of a prosperous southern business man—a long wooden-looking black overcoat and non-committal black hat. He was beautifully shaved; his eyes were unusually alert, and he had, I remember, a strangely pink-and-white skin. Polite and unsmiling, he lent our melodramatic encounter an air of grave propriety. Hands were shaken: bows were exchanged. Amid a murmur of compliments and thanks we set out to see the puppet-show.

We found it at the bottom of a narrow, rutted, unpaved, almost unlighted lane, full of inquisitive onlookers and predatory children. Without an escort, our car might have lost its tyres, and we should certainly have had some uncomfortable moments arriving and departing. As it was, the crowd divided quietly in front of us, re-formed decorously behind us and, since the performance had been arranged for our especial benefit, gradually flooded in to occupy the empty seats at the rear of the theatre, where they remained absorbed and appreciative until the final curtain went down. The Sicilian puppet-theatre is genuinely popular art: no genius has ever arisen to lift it from the primitive level. It remains the occupation of large industrious families who paint the back-cloths, stitch the clothes and hammer out the armour, handle the puppets and supply the throats they speak through. Every detail is carefully stylised—the backgrounds

49

against which the drama is played, with their conventionalised castles and palaces (reminiscent of the architectural ornamentation of an English canal-barge) and their stiffly regular garden walks: the trappings that the puppets wear: the tone of voice used to distinguish each separate class of personage. Distressed heroines affect a dulcet bleat or twitter, heroic knights a magniloquent bellow, rising and falling in sonorous southern cadences, villains and ogres a hoarse terrific *fee-fi-fo-fum*. The puppets themselves are elaborately appointed, their swords, helmets, breastplates and greaves of brightly polished beaten tin; and, when armoured warrior meets armoured warrior, swinging and lungeing across the stage at the end of the long iron rods with which the handlers manage them, the clash of their furious collision—for each is the size of a well-grown child of seven or eight—echoes around the theatre walls. Commonplace realism is never attempted; and the surging movement with which the actors advance—usually head-foremost, while their unjointed legs trail out behind—makes them appear to be swimming or flying rather than walking upon solid ground. The speeches they endlessly deliver are spoken in a dialect intelligible only to a Sicilian audience.

Concern with the doings of Charlemagne's paladins may seem odd in the slums of a crowded modern coastal city: it is less strange among the villages and hill-towns of the lonely central regions. All peasant life strikes the urban intruder as cold and bare and melancholy; but the world of the Sicilian peasant has a peculiar air of grimness, owing partly to the character of the people themselves—many of them dark inheritors of Saracen and Carthaginian blood—partly to the conditions that govern their daily life and labour. The landscape they inhabit is lonely and yet overcrowded; for it contains few small villages and, except here and there, where Mussolini's land-reforms have had some effect, fewer single farmhouses. Driven by the age-old fear of rapine and brigandage, the peasant-farmers usually congregate in isolated hill-settlements, from which they ride forth at the hour of dawn and to which they ride back again when twilight is descending. At day-break they slowly invade the fields: from the clump of yellow-grey houses upon a windy hill-top a long silent procession of families takes the tortuous downhill road, blankets pulled over their heads, everything they need for the day strapped to the crupper or piled in the cart that follows them, one after another deserting the line and jogging off into the open country. Darkness approaches, and the procession re-assembles, group succeeding family group, around carts nearly submerged beneath mountainous loads of brushwood, but each a distinct unit, separate and self-absorbed. Most of the men carry a shot-gun slung across their shoulders; and, as a tall mule shies at the car-lamps and plunges suddenly towards the side of the road, sharp ears pricked with terror and glassy eyeballs starting, the cloaked rider, rigid in the saddle, looks momentarily as aloof and romantic as Rembrandt's Polish Cavalier.

The same air of pride and separateness is perceptible in the gravely strolling crowds of a Sicilian village-square or main-street. The crowd, as in a North African city, is predominantly masculine; but the colour of its clothing is sable instead of dingy white. In some regions the cloaks that the peasants carry are made of dark-blue ribbed velvet, handed down from father to son till they are almost inky-black with use and age; and I was told by a young man, owner of some property in a remote central district where agrarian unrest was prevalent, that when he set out one evening under armed guard to attend a local conclave, peasant after peasant stepped from the track, raising his cloak on his arm to conceal the lower part of his face, thus warning the passers-by of his formal anonymity and dissociating himself from any trouble that might occur during the next few hours. My informant added that the effect was chilling; and his adventure, he explained, had taken place near Enna, a hill-city equally sad and ancient, in which from an earlier visit, while it was still called Castrogiovanni, I remembered having plumbed the depths of gloom and loneliness. Perhaps I had been unlucky in the day I chose, a cold but clear Spring afternoon. Dusk was beginning to swamp the landscape, running down from the crevices of the hills, advancing with the long shadows of the acropolis on which the city perches; and all around "the Navel of Sicily"—for Enna is the midmost point of the whole Sicilian land-mass—swept the desolate rise-and-fall of tawny naked mountain-flanks, with an angle of Persephone's sacred lake shining cold and faraway. Enna was a home of the cult of Demeter—not of the kindly corn-goddess whom Grecian settlers worshipped, but of the Black Demeter revered by the indigenous Sikels, horse-headed divinity of the earth and underworld; and on the edge of the town there is a flight of steps and a rough quadrangular altar clumsily carved from the native black volcanic rock, a sanctuary being used as a public latrine when last I visited Castrogiovanni.

Tufa, or pumice-stone, quarried from the hill, was also the substance employed by mediaeval and seventeen-century architects. The surface of the buildings looks coarse and dark and gritty; and I recollect wandering in a trance of depression through dark and narrow thoroughfares, past small dark-visaged Baroque churches, occasionally pausing at the dim threshold of some exiguous drinking-place, which enclosed three or four old men, hatted and cloaked, seated silently together beneath a single electric-light bulb. Old women, dark-shawled, slipped in and out of a church-door. The hotel was bad and expensive; and as night fell the surrounding obscurity seemed to be flooding-in through every crevice, rising from the gulf of darkness below, borne on the gusts of the icy plangent night-wind. Yet, if Enna is a focus of primitive gloom—situated close to the gate of Hades whither gloomy Dis in his chariot hurried the reluctant Corn Maiden—it owes much of its desolation to merely human agencies. Here as elsewhere the forests have been cut down, and goats have stripped and destroyed the tender hopeful new growth. Sulphur, a mainstay of Sicilian industry, is now mined beside the Lake of Enna. But in classical times the whole valley was cele-brated for its richness. Hounds were reputed to lose the scent, confused by the exquisite effluvium of meadows, flowers and blossoming shrubs; "bronze-rustling"* corn-fields yielded a hundred-fold, and the rocky stronghold of Chthonian Demeter surveyed the labyrinths of a huge garden dedicated to Persephone.

The luxuriance of central Sicily has vanished with its wood-lands. To recover that richness one must follow the coast; for, whereas the mountains of the centre, like their inhabitants, have an almost northern gravity—the flowers that grow by the road are usually hedges of woody wild geranium—the broad coastal plains round Palermo and Catania are full of lemon-yards and orange-groves, mixed with silvery plantations of the far more ancient olive. Lemon, orange and cactus were all introduced to Sicily by its Arab conquerors; both the fruits are said to have come from India, from those fantastic countries lying towards the sunrise which inflamed the imagination of the landlocked Mediterranean peoples; and, as they burden the branches among their flowers and foliage, both still keep something of their mysterious and romantic quality. While the orange belongs to the sun, the lemon's charm is lunar, its rind being pale and cool and smooth, the colour of moonshine during the hottest summer

* Pindar calls Demeter *Chalkokrotos* or "bronze-rustling", an epithet that puzzled commentators suppose must refer to her more savage Chthonian aspects. But may it not have been suggested by the metallic shudder of the wind travelling across a field of ripe corn?

months, its waxen blossoms having a pervasive scent that brings a suggestion of midnight into the heat and glare of midday. The orange by comparison seems to burn with inward warmth. Yet the colours that its globe assumes remain extremely various, ranging from a mild and delicate yellow to a fierce and dusky copper-red. The orange-groves around Catania include an immense acreage of dark-leaved trees, laden with oranges of many shapes and colourings; and wherever the orange-trees go they are followed by a peculiar weed which grows so densely and rapidly that it soon overwhelms and obliterates other vegetation. Its name we were unable to learn—a peasant, working in the garden, vaguely referred to it as *un fiore*; but it bears small flowers of a pallid saffron shade, and its long succulent green-white stalks creak and crunch beneath the footsteps. What a setting for idyllic love! Dark-foliaged, ruddy-fruited, the laden trees are everywhere—a garden of the Hesperides, trackless, endless, undisturbed. Underfoot, musically resilient, the most welcoming of natural beds . . .

Sicily, after all, was the birthplace of Theocritus—hence the remote fountain-head of European pastoral poetry; and, though Theocritus wrote of Sicilian shepherds amid the cosmopolitan confusion of new-built Alexandria, in the shadow of the half-barbaric court of Ptolemy Philadelphus, the landscapes he evoked were not altogether dream-stuff. In Spring at least there are the flowers to recall him. Plants, it is true, like trees and human beings, have their seasons of decline and historical vicissitudes, appearing in one country, disappearing in another, scattered across fresh territories while they vanish from their birthplaces; and many of the flowers we picked on our journey may have reached his native island since Theocritus left home and set sail for Cos and Egypt; but the embroidery of a Sicilian Spring still suggests his Idylls—those recollections of his innocent youth

54

before he traversed the threshold of the Alexandrian literary world and joined the competitive crowd in the Museum's marble lecture-rooms. Theocritus was a citizen of Syracuse; towards the end of his existence he is said to have returned there; and the stone-walled fields between Syracuse and Noto are starred and spangled with innumerable blossoms springing as close and as thick as in the flowery background of some mediaeval tapestry.

Perhaps most beautiful—certainly most classical in their beauty—are the wild anemones. There are anemones red and blue, the red smaller and black-centred, with diminutive blood-red petals of a peculiar glistening silkiness; marigolds, buttercups and dwarf snapdragon: gaunt asphodel and hispid borage: mallows of a splendid Tyrian purple: gentian-blue speedwell and creeping miniature sweet-pea: besides a tall and impressive plant, later identified as monkshood, which showed large grey thickly-furred leaves and big fantastic yellow flowers, each in the shape of a curling lip and deep overarching monastic cowl. Anemones, mallows and asphodel properly belong to the Theocritean landscape. The author of the *Idylls* was an unwilling town-dweller devoted to the country; and, in spite of his affection for country pursuits which caused Robert Frost, a distinguished exponent of modern pastoral poetry, to declare that he would rather meet Theocritus at a dinner-table than any other dead writer, one must not attempt too close an identification of the classical and the romantic, or the Greek and the English, points of view. The plants and the flowers mentioned by an Hellenic poet are seldom celebrated for their own sake, as they are celebrated again and again by Shakespeare and Herrick, Blake, Wordsworth, Shelley, Keats and Gerard Manley Hopkins—with a sense that the flower is a life in itself, exquisite problem and perpetually disturbing challenge to the human eye that focuses it. No, they are appropriate adornments of the rustic scene, decorative reminders of some mythical tale concerning gods and demigods, or links in a garland to be woven about the beloved's brow. Homer and Sappho are, no doubt, exceptions; but Theocritus' nostalgia for meadows and mountains and caves was singularly devoid of romantic or pantheistic feeling.

Such emotions arise during the latest periods of literature, also during the earliest. Art may recover its youth through sophistication, as did European writing and painting in the nine-teenth-century; but the sophistication of Alexandria seems at this time to have been peculiarly deadening, and to have produced a tyranny of critical taste by which literature was held in immense regard, but any attempt at original literary creation was subjected, as soon as it appeared, to the most harsh and jealous scrutiny. Callimachus was the arbiter of literary decorum; and, since he himself was incapable of prolonged poetic effort, he discouraged length in others and austerely announced that a great book was a great evil. Besides, the taste of the period, though scholars might struggle to preserve its purity, was by no means uncontaminated. Alexander's unification of Greece and subjugation of the in-dependent city-states in which the Greek genius had achieved its earliest flowering, had been a prelude to his conquest of the East, over which he had ranged like the Indian Dionysus; and already the influence of Eastern modes had begun to lie heavy on European culture. His successors were Eastern monarchs; and, while Theocritus lived and wrote in Egypt, Ptolemy Philadelphus followed the Egyptian custom of taking to wife his own sister Arsinoë. Ptolemy's coronation banquet was a triumph of Asiatic opulence, the imagery of Hellenic myth being presented in a setting of Syrian or Persian splendour, with interminable pageants of gods and goddesses, satyrs, sileni, maenads, bacchantes, wood-nymphs and sixteen hundred garlanded boys, following a refulgent parade of gold and silver vessels, the whole procession winding its way past the dining-couches of the favoured guests, beneath white-and-scarlet awnings, among innumerable decorative trophies, banks of laurel and myrtle, and exhibitions of statuary by celebrated Old Masters, across a carpet of lilies and roses, brought in mid-winter from the royal hot-houses. But the chief fascination of the show was its vulgar realism—the voluptuous verisimilitude of the mythological scenes enacted. Many of the statues even were observed to be "wearing real clothes".

Apart from the courtly compliments he was sometimes obliged to pay, Theocritus' verse contains numerous reflections of his Alexandrian background. Thus in the famous Fifteenth Idyll, he describes the domestic existence of two prosperous and frivolous married women, Praxinoë and Gorgo, natives of Syracuse but adopted citizens of the Egyptian capital, setting out with child and slave-girl to admire a religious spectacle arranged by Queen Arsinoë, and gossiping as they go about their improvident, possessive and drably unattractive husbands. In their veils and shawls and fashionable hats, they suggest Tanagra figurines possessed of speech and movement. They swear by "Our Lady" —the goddess Persephone; but the deity whose festival they visit is the Syrian god Adonis; and, when with incessant chatter they have edged their way along the crowded streets, through a dense throng of carriages and cloaked and booted officers, and have been frightened by the passing of the King's caparisoned war-horses, they find themselves at last in a sumptuous Eastern mortuary chamber, where the dead god is lying in state amid censers of gold and miniature gardens "arrayed in silver baskets", under a bower of foliage on which the young loves perch like nightingales, while a celebrated foreign singer begins to intone the funeral dirge.

Praxinoë and Gorgo seem perfectly at ease—they are all un-critical admiration of the show provided; but, an ill-tempered stranger having begged them to desist from their "interminable cooing talk", and from boring him to death with thier "eternal broad vowels," they retort angrily that they are "ladies of Syracuse," and that Dorian women, they suppose, can lawfully speak with a Doric accent. Theocritus himself may have kept his Sicilian brogue. At least he was never completely acclimatised, never lost his poetic identity in the rôle of cosmopolitan *littérateur*, but, just as Housman continued to draw sustenance from the distant regions of an unforgotten past, still nourished his imagination on the landscape he had left behind. He was one of the first of the homeless poets—a type soon to grow increasingly common in European literature. Almost every poet of our own age has been to some extent an exile—romantic wanderer, spiritual outcast or wild bohemian vagabond; and it is difficult now to imagine a condition of society such as existed in the Mediterranean world before the modern metropolis over-whelmed the ancient city-state, and the pressure of a polyglot crowd destroyed the poet's feeling of companionship with his fellow citizens. Theocritus occupied a midway place, balanced between old and new; and his return to Syracuse, if in fact he returned, is a subject that should receive the attention of some reflective story-teller. During his absence how had the city changed? Did he settle down, like Shakespeare at Stratford, to enjoy the prosaic comforts of a local adventurer who had made good? Or, finding the landscapes he carried in his memory more beautiful than the fields and mountain-slopes that he at length revisited, merely exchange the solitude of Egypt for a deeper sense of dispossession?

IV

EVERY TRAVELLER AND every student of travel-
books—everyone, indeed, whose visions of what might be occasionally colour his observations of what so lamentably is—has been
visited now and then by glimpses of the Ideal City: not the City of
God but a city of men, where human dignity and love of order and
man's affection for his own species have found expression and
justification through the labours of the architect. Many actual
towns seem to embody a reflection of this ideal metropolis—
Vicenza, perhaps, or Bath: or, in their diminutive and unambitious
way, such English country towns as Blandford or Bradford-on-
Avon. But among modern races, particularly the races of the
North, beauty in any shape is beset with many dangers: squalid
suburbs have been allowed to proliferate around the ancient
nucleus: streets have been widened and "improved", gimcrack
shop-fronts run up: finally enemy bombers, in search of some
semi-mythical "marshalling-yard"—the military objective usually
invoked when beautiful buildings are to be laid low—have broken
the symmetry of crescent, avenue and market-square.

Yet the vision remains: the aspiration persists. And there are few
places in Southern Europe where one feels so close to fulfilment

as in the enchanting town of Noto, which lies some twenty-five miles along the coastal road from Syracuse. The effect it produces is equally harmonious and homogeneous; for, after the destructive earthquake of 1693, its citizens abandoned the original site and decided to re-establish themselves in a less ill-omened neighbourhood. Thus Noto is the achievement of a single period, and bears the mark throughout of the same creative impulse. It is the centre, incidentally, of a wealthy agricultural district whose cultivators could afford the expense of noble and elaborate planning; and in the new project they evidently determined to allow their taste the widest scope, constructing for their own delectation the perfect small metropolis. The result was a genuine city, with all the urbanity of the metropolitan character, yet far enough from political high-roads to preserve a certain quietude. Its architects had a further advantage. Nearby quarries provided abundant material—a yellow limestone harder and closer-grained than is to be found in other parts of Sicily. The colour of this stone is a delicate warm-hued golden-buff; and among the dark foliage of squares and gardens, against the crystalline azure of a Spring sky, churches and palaces give an extraordinary impression of liveliness and lightness.

Coming from the north, the traveller passes beneath an eagle-surmounted triumphal arch, then enters a long thoroughfare full of splendid buildings. Noto is placed on a gentle slope, its side-streets running up and down, bisected by the straight line of a spacious central artery. Here are the Cathedral, the bigger churches, many imposing private houses. All have an unmistakable air of grandeur, whether one is considering the Cathedral itself, raised high above its surroundings on a terrace approached by three gradual flights of steps, or the small palace that confronts it from the opposite side of the main street. This palace, the ancestral home of the Landolina family, is an elegant single-storeyed edifice, more French than Italian in style, with a high-pillared arcade encompassing the inner structure. Every building has a separate charm, and there is never a suspicion of lifeless uniformity. The inspiration is, of course, Baroque; but in Noto the Baroque mannerism has taken an oddly individual turn. It is so chaste as to be almost classical, without any of the wanton exuberance that distinguishes the productions of most Baroque architects, for example in the churches of Trapani, or in Acireale and other cities of the east coast. Few statues appear on façades: no ranks of gesticulating saints are poised above the pediments: but for the rhetoric of monumental sculpture the architect has substituted the poetry of correct proportions, often leaving his niches tenantless, allowing his master-plan to speak for itself, uniting Baroque enthusiasm to a Palladian sense of form, and from the combination evolving a design of impressive breadth and dignity.

Yet the dignity of the result does not exclude lightheartedness. To describe the fascination of a building is as difficult as to pin down the beauty of a famous dancer's movements, since an attempt at technical analysis must leave out of account the living quality of the dancer's or the architect's skill. It must be enough to say that these masterpieces of classical Baroque often reveal a charming linear fantasy, and that, whereas some façades are gracefully incurved, others swell out like sails of stone obeying the propulsion of a soft wind. Buildings, moreover, are ingeniously juxtaposed, so that the idiom of one affords a stimulating contrast to the idiom employed by its immediate neighbour— an exchange of compliments or parade of competitive grace that never goes beyond the limits of architectural good manners. There is a look of amity about the monuments of Noto, particularly refreshing after the strident discord of the average twentieth-century skyline.

I have mentioned the exquisite colour of the local stone; and such is its durability that there has been little crumbling and blurring of the original mason-work. Ornamentation is notably sparse; but what ornament the architects decided to confer—around a niche, above a doorway or along a balcony—remains almost as sharp and clear as the day that a mason's chisel first extricated it from the golden block. More than two hundred years of history have left Noto strangely youthful; and during our visit it was crowded with children—not the swarthy changelings of many Sicilian cities, but fair-complexioned, light-haired children who might have been bred in an English village or a country town of Northern France. They swarmed and chattered around us—up the steps to the Cathedral, over the symmetrically-laid cobbles of ascending and descending side-streets which usually ended in some well-proportioned minor church. Crossing its threshold, we entered a new world; for, while the exterior had a Palladian reserve, its interior decoration seemed to anticipate the happier products of the Rococo genius. Golden without, it was a dazzling white within, pillars, arches, chapels and roof immaculate with candid stucco, over an arch teased into bat-winged scrolls, or gathered into a richly decorative motif to support some latticed balcony, from which a choir of unseen nuns had once discoursed aerial music . . .

Noto is a city that stands alone; but not far away to the west there are other Baroque towns that run it very close indeed. Ispica and Modica are both rewarding places; and Ragusa, perched on the lip of a limestone ravine, which is terraced with gardens and orchards, and pitted with the mouths of ancient rock-tombs, has an incomparably beautiful situation. Seen from across the gulf it is romantic and appealing as only a hill-town can be, whether glimpsed from a modern motor-road or emergent in the golden distance of a picture by Giovanni Bellini. Nor, when one has entered it, does Ragusa, unlike many towns of the same kind, lose its fascination. Though architecturally not so complete as Noto, it contains at least one delightful assemblage of late-seventeenth-century buildings—the broad avenue that leads to the great Basilica di S. Giorgio, a Jesuit church justly described in an Italian guide-book as *"una delle più felici espressioni del barocco siciliano"*, which looks obliquely down its stretch. This avenue is lined with two-storeyed palaces of the same epoch; and there is something about their sun-baked solidity, the row of spreading palm trees planted along the middle of the street, and the tawny bulk of the church upon which every line converges, that recalls a similar perspective in Southern Spain or Mexico. The Iberian influence seems particularly strong; and a Spanish strain, the historians assure us, forms an important part of the Sicilian heritage.

That strain made for sumptuous solemnity. Elsewhere, in the churches of Noto and in a variety of monuments in or near Palermo, the manifestations of the Baroque genius had a gayer, livelier colouring. Art is, among other things, a product of the pride of life; and personally I have an affection for artists whose love of life, and of the world of appearances, has fought a winning battle against that "horror of life" which the noblest of French nineteenth-century poets declared that he had also experienced since his earliest childhood. Such an artist was Giacomo Serpotta. If the pride of Rubens' and the gaiety of Renoir's spirit, their sensuous appreciation of the glory of the flesh, was mixed-in with their pigments, Serpotta accomplished the somewhat more unusual feat of translating his pride and gaiety into terms of plasterwork. Of all the artists who have handled stucco, none shows a more fruitful invention, a lighter, more fluid touch, a more appealing sense of natural beauty. But his sense of beauty was regulated and disciplined by an uncommonly exacting sense

63

of form. There was nothing about Serpotta of the naive provincial craftsman. His talent was essentially urbane; and this urbanity is the more surprising since he seldom or never stirred beyond his native province, and executed his best work within the confines of a single city. To Palermo he left his masterpieces, and in Palermo he was content to enjoy the fame those masterpieces brought him. Evidently a sensible, well-balanced man: and so indeed one would have deduced from the portrait-head which stands in the pleasant cloister-gallery outside the Oratorio di S. Lorenzo. Here is a shrewd, dignified, good-natured face that might have belonged to one of the French Encyclopaedists. His neckcloth and wig are plain but neat. On the pedestal of the effigy are merely his name and numerals indicating that he was born in 1656 and died in 1732. Other information about Serpotta is sparse and hard to come by; the ordinary English guidebooks do not condescend to mention him; while an Italian guide lists several Serpottas, no doubt his brothers or sons, who may have collaborated in his ambitious designs, as did Tiepolo's family in the preparation of his frescoes. But Giacomo was clearly the chief designer, and each decorative scheme bears the signature of an extremely individual genius.

Sometimes that signature appears on the walls of private palaces; for the Palermitan upper classes were rich and cultivated, and in their town and in their country houses maintained an existence of royal prodigality; but Serpotta's finest surviving works are all associated with some religious edifice—the Oratorio di S. Lorenzo or the yet more fantastic and impressive Oratorio di S. Cita, neither of them a well-known building and both hidden away down quiet, ancient back-streets. In each Serpotta's exuberant gifts have been devoted to a comparatively small space—small, that is to say, by comparison with the vast naves and lofty side-chapels of most Sicilian churches; but the

1 3   PALERMO: *Street market*

14 *PALERMO: Oratorio di S. Cita by Giacomo Serpotta*

space he attacked has been filled completely, and the entire
oratory from ceiling to ground-level, and from entrance-door to
altar-piece, has been remodelled in a similar mood. The Oratorio
di S. Cita, as the stranger of the two, should perhaps be first
examined. According to an Italian guide-book, Serpotta worked
here at intervals from 1686 to 1718—"a diversity of epochs . . .
which explains the stylistic discord of the present modelling";
its ornamentation, continues the Italian writer, is *"barocchissima,
prodigiosamente fantasiosa e originale"*—a description that seems
sufficiently just, though the previous reference to "stylistic discord" is neither fair nor accurate. True, the scheme is pro-
digiously bold; statuary large and small, motifs in high and low
relief, are thrown together in a bewilderingly complex pattern
of bodies, scrolls and draperies; but the rhythm of the design is
never broken, and every detail responds to and carries on
another. We are conscious of a general harmony long before we
attempt an analysis of the component features.

The whole interior surface is richly embellished; but it was
on the rear wall, opposite the altar, that Serpotta executed his
most remarkable feats of taste and virtuosity. That wall depicts,
in a stylised and emblematic fashion, the Battle of Lepanto, with
a panel giving a view of the fight, trophies of Turkish arms, and
two adolescent supporters in the guise of ragged war orphans.
The Virgin is enthroned in a panel above; and there are four
complementary panels depicting scenes of sacred history. But
now observe the device by which these scenes, deeply set in
quadrangular frames, are presented to the faithful. As in the
strange roof-top vision accorded to the Apostle Peter, a sheet
has been let down from Heaven, upheld around the edges by a
score of agile *putti*, who struggle with the cumbersome but
delicate stuff, vanish beneath its swags but come bravely thrusting
out again. The wrinkles and folds of the heavenly fabric,

65

represented with a loving naturalism that indicates at the same time its softness and its heaviness, form the background of the six panels which the *putti*, among their other tasks, are balancing and steadying. Every moulded frame encloses a sculptural group in miniature, a dramatic episode complete in itself, having the charm and the meticulous distinction of some celestial peepshow.

Characteristic of Serpotta's art is the assurance with which several different scales are managed simultaneously. Thus, while the *putti* are of realistic dimensions, the supporters beneath the central panel have been considerably reduced to fit the space they occupy, and the height of the figures in the panels is barely five or six inches. Even more diminutive is the prospect of the Battle of Lepanto, with the Virgin in the sky above interceding for her devotees, and the lateen-sails of the galleys below filling, rank behind rank, the gulf between two rocky headlands. The foremost galleys are portrayed in the round; and here, as in the companion pieces, a false perspective has been contrived by the ingenious employment of upward-sloping and converging lines. With variety of scale goes variety of surface. Whereas some motifs are in undulant low relief, many figures lean out from the design robustly three-dimensional, and others again are completely detached, as if they symbolised three stages of some vast creative process, the plaster being the primitive clay from which the works of the creator were gradually emerging—rudimentary yet rhythmic shapes and half-formed heavenly presences, at last the perfect human form, serene and mysteriously smiling upon its coign or window-ledge.

To these detached figures one most often returns. Evidently they are offshoots of the Baroque tradition; but, if they inherit the fantasy of the Baroque spirit, they have no share in its violence. Buildings are sometimes compared to ships; and across the façade, and along the skyline, of a Baroque church its statues stand congregated like energetic passengers, frenziedly waving the vessel on, extending their garments in the manner of pinions and wrestling against the sea-wind, as they signal the distant shore with wildly upraised arms and eyes. A similar enthusiasm pervades the statues that line the nave and chancel; for they are participants in a tremendous drama, and the zest of the Counter-Reformation is still awake within them. Serpotta's religious convictions must remain a matter of doubt; we may assume that he was safely orthodox; but the religious passions of the seventeenth century must have been measurably attenuated by the time they reached his soul. They made little impression on his creative method, which reveals fantasy without fanaticism, and exuberance, tinged by extravagance, without a trace of pious rhetoric.

His was a worldly and cheerful faith—one suited to the peace and wealth of a settled, rich community. How prosperous and calm it was we deduce from the succession of noble country houses, some still inhabited, some derelict and half in ruins, which star the landscape around Palermo. Life passed between a villa at Bagheria and a palace near the Quattro Canti can scarcely have been conducive to the ascetic virtues; and Serpotta's art reflects his society and period, with the modifications imposed by his individual temperament. For luxury is not always gay, nor prosperity attractive; and, while few artists are averse from ease and comfort, the artist, as he absorbs the pleasures of the passing moment, has the knack of reducing them to their essential residue, a distillation of happiness which far outlasts the present day. Women and children crowd Serpotta's designs. Sicilian children—at least in those districts where a northern influence predominates over the darker, gloomier Saracenic strain—are particularly lively and comely, impertinent and uninhibited; and the putti whom Serpotta moulded bear no resemblance to the conventionalised infants of the average Italian sculptor's repertory.

67

Nor do their mothers and sisters conform to a conventional type; and, although they represent Moral Qualities and improving Arts and Sciences, their sensuous and human aspect never disappears beneath the emblematic costume. Charity is the gentlest of human mothers: Fortitude (whom I must later attempt to describe) gives the rôle to which the sculptor has assigned her an astonishingly feminine and entirely unheroic turn.

In the decorative scheme of the Oratorio di S. Lorenzo, a somewhat more formal production than the Oratorio di S. Cita, Serpotta builds up a complex design with equal grace and mastery. The effect is opulent but never ponderous. Details are fantastically elaborate; yet the designer avoids any air of gimcrack ostentation. Wanting the varied splendours of metal, wood and polished stone, plaster is a difficult material, which may look cold without dignity, and fragile and impermanent without the charm of delicacy. But Serpotta's plasterwork is always intensely alive, as if the inward warmth of the artist's imagination had penetrated and transfigured it, giving to each shape a separate existence, dwelling delightedly on the resilient smoothness of flesh, the airiness of floating draperies, the crisp definition of acanthus-leaf or scallop-shell. Variety of surface takes the place of colouring; and, whereas large expanses of unbroken white are often bleak and frigid, Serpotta, using a monumental scale, gives as much subtlety to the gradations of white as did Oudry in his famous picture, aided, of course, by the southern sunshine, which fills his interiors with a dusty luminous haze and falls in long shafts through wide and high-set windows, glancing over the plump flanks of wrestling or embracing *putti*, and striking the shoulder and breast of an attendant angel.

His angels have most of them a curious family likeness, and belong to the same enchanting family as Fortitude and Modesty and Astronomy, and other projections of virtue and wisdom

whom Serpotta enthroned in niches or pinnacled on sumptuous
ornamental brackets, to look down from either side of the nave
upon the throng of worshippers. But, although they are lifted
over the heads of the crowd, these sympathetic and beguiling
personages seem half inclined to join it. Here and there, dis-
daining the fashions prescribed by contemporary neo-classicism,
they are wearing the dresses of the late seventeenth or early
eighteenth century—panniered skirts, stiffly embroidered bodices,
feathers crowning their hair and ruffles at their elbows. In body
they are tall and slender; and in movement—for all are extremely
animated—they produce a peculiar impression of suppleness and
fluency. Had Serpotta a model he loved? Or was he, throughout
his life, haunted by a visionary idea of physical perfection?
Certainly Botticelli's virgins and angels are not more recog-
nisably Botticellian than Serpotta's figures, in their worldlier
way, are unmistakably creations of the Sicilian stuccoist's fancy.
Their mouths are small: their noses are straight: cheeks full and
smooth run down with the line of the jaw towards a neatly-
pointed chin: their expressions are sensuous and feline, the
shadow of a provocative smile sometimes hovering about the lips
and eyes. Typical is the image of Fortitude. With her right hand
poised on her hip brushing back her over-skirt, she is a young
woman in a new dress who has burst into the sculptor's studio
and, striking a pose and turning on her heel, demands that he
admire it. She swings her draperies, exhibits her profile.
Twisting her serpentine neck, she sights along her shoulder,
while the ostrich plumes nod from her head, and the scarf to
which she has attached them wreathes around her left arm . . .
"*The pride of the peacock is the glory of God; The lust of the goat is
the bounty of God . . . The nakedness of woman is the work of God*",
William Blake was to declare in one of the simplest and boldest
of his prophetic utterances. The vanity of woman, Giacomo

Serpotta would appear to have considered, being yet another manifestation of the divine abundance, was not unworthy to be represented within a Christian temple.

V

Norman Invaders—the Conquest of Palermo—Norman and Moorish fashions—Roger I—Silk-weaving and the art of Mosaic—Byzantine Influence—the Capella Palatina—Monreale—the Palazzo Zisa—Nelson at La Favorita

In the closing years of the eleventh century, a first locust-horde of Crusaders drifted across Central Europe to the majestic gates of Constantinople. The Greek Emperor, Alexius Comnenos, persuaded them to accept a free passage into the territory of the Seljuk Turks who, as he had expected and, no doubt, hoped, expeditiously disposed of them; but for several decades wave after wave of pious desperadoes continued to vex the Eastern Empire, astonishing the Greeks by their rapacity, vulgarity and rugged northern insolence. Determined not to be overawed, their *parvenu* leaders stormed and sprawled around the great imperial throne-rooms; and, while his companions were addressing their host, one knight ascended the vacant throne and lolled his ugly length there. The Emperor's attitude was carefully diplomatic. He temporised and flattered and out-manoeuvred. But more than a hundred years later, in April 1204, the whole weight of the Fourth Crusade was diverted against the sacred city: Baldwin of Flanders and Bonifacio of Montferrat, aided to his eternal disgrace by the Venetian Doge Enrico Dandolo, assaulted Constantinople from land and sea, burst through its ill-manned ramparts, and looted or destroyed the splendid accumulation of nearly nine triumphant centuries. Its citizens were enslaved or slaughtered: prostitutes danced or plied their trade on the high altar of the Church of the Holy Wisdom: eikons and church vestments were cut to pieces for their gold and precious stones: the imperial tombs were violated, Justinian's body being tumbled from its coffin and stripped of its costly wrappings: surviving masterpieces of classical sculpture were melted down to provide the army with bronze and silver coinage. Having thus vindicated the superiority of the northern breed, not a few of the crusading chieftains quietly returned home.

Meanwhile, during roughly the same period, another band of northern adventurers was adapting itself very differently to the Mediterranean way of life. Since 902, when they captured Taormina, the Muslims had held Sicily, and had made Palermo an Arab metropolis renowned throughout the civilised world. Their architects filled the rich surrounding plain, the famous *Conca del Oro*, with palaces, pavilions and kiosks, set in an immense arabesque pattern of vineyards, gardens, fishponds. Then the Christian adventurers arrived. By 1060 Robert Guiscard and his brothers, penniless but energetic offspring of Tancred of Hauteville, an undistinguished Norman squire, had conquered and consolidated large holdings on the Italian mainland and were looking towards Sicily, which Norman troops had already visited at the invitation of a Byzantine general some twenty years earlier. In 1071 they entered Palermo;* but, unlike the Christian knights who were soon to sack Jerusalem and, subsequently, ravish Constantinople, they assumed control of the Arab city with very

---

* The Arabs exhibited their courage by leaving the city gates open; and, before the final assault, a Norman knight, not to be outdone in hardihood, is said to have galloped across Palermo carrying his lance at rest.

little bloodshed. They were themselves conquered by the Sicilian climate, by the warmth and fragrance of the Golden Shell, and by the civilisation, compact of leisure, learning, luxury, that Byzantines and Arabs had built up within its mountainous rim. The Normans remained a bellicose people; but they discovered that second only to the crafts of war and government was the delicious art of wasting time.

Of the various historical epochs that have left their mark on modern Palermo, the Norman age is the most absorbing. True, there are the memorials of Baroque art and architecture—the oratories that Serpotta designed and the impressive palaces of the Palermitan aristocracy (nowadays, alas, much damaged by Allied bombs and gun-fire), besides their houses in the country round, including the nightmare villa of the eccentric Prince Palagonia who, apparently in order to intimidate his wife, surrounded that graceful crescent-shaped edifice with a private army of grotesque figures which mop and mow across the garden and scowl obscenely from the garden walls. There are also traces of Spanish occupation, and many relics of the Middle Ages: among which none is stranger and bolder than the terrifying *Triumph of Death* that once stood in the arcaded courtyard of the Palazzo Sclafani. Here the Pale Horse monopolises attention—a gaunt monster of a horse, nearly skeletonious, with empty eye-sockets, starting neck-tendons, and ribs that seem to saw its hide; from which Death, the omnipotent huntsman, has just directed his tremendous shaft against the startled crowd beneath its hooves—those worldly prelates, dissolute lovers and gay and thoughtless courtladies dear to the imagination of the mediaeval moralist. The colours of the fresco, usually attributed to a painter of the fifteenth-century Catalan school, are curiously dusky and livid. But neither this painting nor any of the achievements of earlier and later periods produces so deep and durable an effect as certain monuments raised during the Arab-Norman heyday.

For Norman and Arab must share the credit; and their contribution was itself subordinate to the pervasive influence of Byzantine masters. Considering their barbarous origins, it is remarkable that the Norman overlords of Palermo should have learned so rapidly and readily. Yet learn they did; and during the reign of Roger I, Count of Sicily, youngest brother of Robert Guiscard and the last of the family to leave his native farm-lands, and that of Roger II, his second son, crowned in the Cathedral of Palermo on Christmas Day 1130, the city became a fascinating combination of Eastern and Western modes, Catholic, Orthodox and Muslim cultures. This fusion astonished and delighted an erudite Arab traveller who, arriving in Sicily from Spain towards the close of the twelfth century, observed (according to Gregorovius) that the Sicilian monarch not only spoke but wrote in Arabic, that he kept a harem of Eastern women, and was served by eunuchs and pages secretly attached to the Muslim faith. The burgess-wives of Palermo followed Eastern fashions. Rouged and scented, clothed in gold-coloured fabrics, with veils and chains and heavy jewellery, they reminded him in church of a crowd at a mosque, and admiringly he compared them to gazelles and antelopes. Roger II, boldest of his line, had a trusted Saracen body-guard; Greek, Latin, Hebrew and Arabic were the languages employed in his official documents; but for his conception of kingship he turned to Byzantium, modelling his rule on the theocratic absolutism of the Byzantine emperors; and a mosaic depicting his coronation by Christ in S. Maria dell' Ammiraglio shows Roger in massively-embroidered robes, his lean, energetic, bearded northern face beneath the high, angular Byzantine crown, with jewel- and pearl-strung tassels or lappets, already familiar in portraits of the Eastern sovereigns.

It was Roger who, by bringing craftsmen from Greece,

introduced to the West the exquisite art of silk-weaving. Here
again he imitated Byzantium; for, in almost all the impressions that
remain to us of the domestic life of the Eastern court, curtains
and tapestries heighten the effect of circumambient splendour.
Sliding on rings, they are looped gracefully over the heads of
saintly and imperial personages. They shrouded the great Taber-
nacle of S. Sophia, which the Crusaders smashed and carried off;
and, in the airily fantastic architectural backgrounds that
decorate the central dome of the magnificent circular church of
St. George in Salonika's old town, richly-figured curtains add to
the complexity of window, arch and pillared turret. We know
that they encircled the throne itself, and that, when the Emperor
wished to retire, his silent eunuchs immediately drew the veil,
enveloping their master in a silken solitude. Such was the
atmosphere of luxury and inaccessibility that surrounded the
divine ruler. Tesselated pavements shone underfoot; rare
marbles sheathed the walls and gleamed from the convexity of
polished antique columns; mosaics glimmered from the roof; and,
by way of contrast to this assemblage of hard and lustrous surfaces,
soft, variegated, volatile stuffs wavered and undulated against the
sea-breezes, blown in through the open casements from court-
yards and gardens built above the Golden Horn.

Palermo's Norman kings also encouraged the art of Greek
mosaicists. It has been suggested that a native school, which had
once produced for Hiero of Syracuse a state-galley with a mosaic
floor, designed to illustrate the whole story of the *Iliad*, may
perhaps have survived from classical times;* but Roger II, under
Byzantine influence, gave the art a new direction and established
a factory of mosaic-workers in his royal dwelling. They embellished his private rooms, nowadays called the *Stanze di re*

* This theory, however, is treated with some contempt by Otto Demus in
his excellent work, *The Mosaics of Norman Sicily*.

Ruggero; and in the same palace they planned the ornamentation of a sumptuous private chapel. The Capella Palatina is one of the noblest and most immediately moving monuments completed in Southern Europe between the collapse of the Hellenic ideal and the birth of the Renaissance spirit. It is evidently dangerous in any work of art to attempt to distinguish the dominant emotion or aesthetic ruling passion; but, as soon as we have succumbed to the spell of a building or picture, the temptation, however misguided, proves almost irresistible. Ruskin made the attempt again and again; and his eloquent generalisations about *The Nature of Gothic*, though they involved him in numerous errors, are still intensely stimulating. "The vital principle (he wrote) is not the love of *Knowledge*, but the love of *Change*. It is that strange disquietude of the Gothic spirit that is its greatness; that restlessness of the dreaming mind, which wanders hither and thither among the niches, and flickers feverishly around the pinnacles, and frets and fades in labyrinthine knots and shadows along wall and roof, and yet is not satisfied nor shall be satisfied. The Greek could stay in his triglyph furrow, and be at peace; but the work of the Gothic art . . . can neither rest in, nor from, its labour, but must pass on, sleeplessly, until its love of change shall be pacified for ever in the change that must come alike on them that wake and them that sleep." Well, if the Gothic artist was inspired by the love of change, the Byzantine was impelled by the love of order and the worship of stability. But it was not a human order Byzantine artists envisaged, so much as an order founded on divine rule, in which the Emperor himself was the mere earthly counterpart of the Heavenly Ruler, whose "*Thrones, Dominations, Princedoms, Virtues, Powers*" were re-produced by the Byzantine court with its carefully-graded ranks of attendants, circling and ceaselessly ministering through the Imperial presence-chambers.

The Emperor, inevitably, was the centre of the circle; and, though individual monarchs might be dethroned and very often condemned to execution or appalling tortures, their fate did nothing to impair the conception of his sanctity. In a world of flux and decay, with the last remains of the classical order gradually disappearing and barbarians of every race perpetually gnawing away at the foundations of the Christian-Roman empire, he alone in his unconquered city represented permanence. Like his Roman predecessors, he was semi-divine, jewelled and painted and bewigged, seated on a throne that, during one reign at least, was raised by invisible means at the close of an audience and vanished into a room above; and no device was neglected that could increase his prestige. His trappings were of gold and white and purple; "Silentiaries", carrying golden rods, piloted a foreign visitor through the elaborate ceremonies of introduction; and even the white-robed eunuchs who surrounded him have been compared to angels, raising their large sleeves to shield their eyes as they approached the central glory. If the Emperor was the image of God, so God was the Celestial Monarch. *Christos Pantokrator* was the aspect of God the Son usually chosen by Byzantine artists—not a deity who pities and comforts and shares in human sufferings, but a sternly impartial Ruler and Legislator come to judge the quick and the dead. Thus Christ appears in the Capella Palatina, at Monreale and at Cefalù; and, while he gazes down from the incurved shell of the apse, his left hand grasping the Gospel, the long fingers of the right raised in solemn benediction, angels and prophets and saints, wearing the splendid apparatus of Byzantine clerics and court officials, stand ranged on lower-wall spaces. Martial angels support the dome— heavenly warriors only less imposing than the wonderful angels in the convent-church of Daphni; and closer to the congregation are the Saints of the Eastern Church, their gravely forbidding features, with high naked bulbous foreheads and cold authoritative suspicious eyes, contracted into expressions of ascetic self-esteem. All these figures, some of them evidently portraits, and the accompanying illustrations of Old and New Testament history, are set off by the refulgent background—*opus vermiculatum*—of glassy-gold mosaic-cubes. The slight unevenness of this greenish-golden ground, above the smooth-worn shafts of the columns and the chequer-work of porphyry, marble and serpentine with which the church is paved and wainscotted, makes its radiance seem doubly rich. It fills the chapel with a luminous obscurity that confuses and yet stimulates. Here, you feel, is a suggestion of the darkness of dogma, irradiated from within by a mysterious glow of faith and hope.

The faith of the Norman sovereigns, however, was not always safely orthodox. Roger II, during whose reign the Capella Palatina was begun, though it would appear to have been completed during the reign of William I, adopted an extremely latitudinarian point of view towards religious problems; and, to symbolise the alliance between East and West, his chapel has a golden honeycomb-roof of Saracenic workmanship, and contains an inscription in Arabic, as well as in Latin and Greek, commemorating the installation of a clock in the year 1142. No Caliph could have been more magniloquent. "THE ORDER (his inscription reads) IS ISSUED BY HIS ROYAL MAJESTY THE MAGNIFICENT RULER, THE EXALTED ONE, TO WHOM MAY GOD GRANT EVERLASTING DAYS AND WHOSE SIGN MAY HE CONFIRM, THAT THIS INSTRUMENT BE CONSTRUCTED FOR RECORDING THE HOURS. IN THE METROPOLIS OF SICILY PROTECTED BY GOD IN THE 536th YEAR." The date given is calculated not from the birth of Christ but from the Hegira of the Prophet. William I, Roger's successor, was so Eastern in his habits and outlook that his disapproving clergy and nobles nicknamed him "William the Bad"; but his son, "William the Good", last of the direct male line of Tancred of Hauteville, did something to redress the balance and, among his other achievements, built on the hill above Palermo the enormous Cathedral of Monreale. I first visited Monreale during the celebration of a High Mass, when, through the long bars of sunlight which slanted down from the clerestory windows, climbed delicate cobweb films of slowly wreathing incense-smoke. Behind the smoke-haze, above the voices and the music, emerged the image of Christ the All-Ruler. Again it monopolises the summit of the apse; and, as the golden concavity swells upwards and outwards, the divine representation which it encloses is distorted yet immensely magnified. The hand that blesses curves round like a crustacean's claw: the impending face, furrowed and bearded, hints at the ancient implacable justice of a God that is not mocked.

By comparison, the atmosphere of the rest of the church is care-free, almost worldly. On a second visit, many years later, I found neither incense-smoke nor devotional music; and, though the Christ in the apse remained as strange and portentous, I felt, when I turned to the body of the church, that I had slipped between the pages of some vast illuminated missal. The effect is diverting and instructive rather than impressive. A triple range of stories-told-in-mosaic pluck the imagination to and fro. There is God the Father with Adam and Eve, in an Eden that consists of three slender trees, umbrella-shaped, brush-shaped, star-shaped. Immediately below them Lot is deserting Sodom; and, as the city subsides into a symmetrical brazier of flames, Lot's wife in Byzantine robes looks regretfully backward. On the same level, to the left, a pair of winged and haloed angels are seated in the house of Lot, while Lot holds off the outrageous Sodomites from his open front-door. Ships set sail across crisp blue seas:

miracles are performed: holy men are martyred . . . It is fair to add that Monreale's mosaic picture-book has probably been much restored; for in November 1811 one of the cathedral choristers put a candle down beside a cupboard and started a blaze which he tried, but failed, to beat out. Whereupon "the little Herostratus" (as Gregorovius pleasantly calls him) decided to close the cupboard and went home hoping for the best. The entire cathedral was nearly consumed; many of the mosaics were partly destroyed; and the roof-timbers, as they fell in, splintered the marble tombs of both William the Good and William the Bad. Nineteenth century efforts to repair the damage, which included the gift of a new roof by King Louis I of Bavaria, have not been very fortunate.

Still, besides some portions of its original mosaic lining, the Cathedral has preserved its ornate and lovely garden-cloisters and its admirable dark-green bronze doors, designed and cast by Bonnanus Civis Pisanus in 1186. From the terrace of the hotel-restaurant you look out over the Conca del Oro, with a wide gulf of the sea directly ahead and the mountains rising on either hand. Below is the site of the pleasure-gardens and summer-palaces, inhabited by successive rulers—the wreckage of La Cuba, built by William II, and to the West, under the foothills of Monte Pellegrino, the Chinese pavilion, erected by Ferdinand IV, to which Nelson, during a somewhat inglorious phase of his career, must have escorted Lady Hamilton. La Cuba is one of the few remaining secular monuments of the Norman-Saracenic heyday: but from the outskirts of modern Palermo rises a formidable quadrangular building known as the Palazzo Zisa, its name being a corruption of the Arabic word for "splendid", half Norman *donjon*, with low vaulted chambers in the thickness of its massive walls, half Moorish pleasure-house. Today the home of Prince Belmonte, a renowned authority on the art and

15 *NOTO: Piazza dell' Immacolata*

16 RAGU

17 THE VILLA
PALAGONI
Bagheria nec
Palermo

architecture of his native island, it includes, among distinctively Northern details, a magnificent Eastern banqueting hall, enriched with circular mosaic plaques of peacocks, trees and huntsmen. The ceiling, like the roof of the Capella Palatina, is fretted into a stalactite pattern; and across the floor, from a fountain in a niche, runs a paved rivulet of clear water. This room originally opened upon a garden courtyard.

The Palazzo Zisa was begun by William I, completed by William II. With William the Good, the male line of Tancred of Hauteville came to an abrupt end; and the Kingdom of Sicily, through Constance, daughter of Roger I, whom he had married to the Emperor Henry VI of Germany, passed to her son, the Emperor Frederick II, crowned in the Cathedral of Palermo at the age of four in 1198. Frederick, however, carried on the tradition of learning, licence and spiritual unorthodoxy initiated by his Norman forbears. "The grandson of Barbarossa . . . successively the pupil, the enemy, and the victim of the church" (as Gibbon describes him with his usual gift of the resounding phrase), he was twice excommunicated; and, when, after twelve years' delay, he had finally agreed to attempt the reconquest of Palestine, lacking Papal sanction he was obliged to crown himself King of Jerusalem before the altar of the Holy Sepulchre. He dazzled and alarmed the contemporary universe. *Stupor Mundi et Immutator Mirabilis*, Frederick kept a court of poets, philosophers and scientists (at which the first sonnet was written and, according to Dante, Italian poetry had its birthplace), encouraged medical research, formed a menagerie of rare animals, mastered six languages, was versed in philosophy and natural history, and composed an important illustrated treatise, *De Arte Venandi cum Avibus*, on the royal art of hawking, a work remarkable for its exact observation of the habits and plumage of wild birds. The Great Khan having demanded that, as a token of

F

submission, the Emperor should join his service, Frederick opined that he might make a very good falconer . . . His religious views were far from conventional, and his treatment of the Pope induced an English historian to coin the curious verb "to Frederize". For crusading he had little taste, since "his liberal sense and knowledge taught him to despise the phantoms of superstition and the crowns of Asia . . . and his ambition was occupied by the restoration of the Italian monarchy from Sicily to the Alps." But Frederick finished life cruel, embittered and disillusioned; and in 1250 his body was brought back to the Cathedral of Palermo. There it was buried in a huge sarcophagus of gleaming wine-dark porphyry, supported on the shoulders of four prodigious lions, beneath a canopy upheld by six antique columns with rich Corinthian capitals.

Physically, Frederick II is said to have been "red, bald and short-sighted", but to have possessed "good features and a pleasing countenance". The tomb of the Emperor was opened in 1781—evidently an impious gesture. Yet who could resist such an opportunity of intruding on the legendary dead? What, for instance, would a biographer not give to have been present when the clergyman of Hucknall Torkard looked down into Byron's coffin—or when a group of officials and antiquaries opened the leaden shell said to have contained King John? On that occasion, I am told by a friend, the inner shell was seen to be filled to the brim with a black and viscous fluid. All retreated in alarm and disgust, till an aged scholar advanced and coolly dipped his finger into it, then placed his finger between his lips, murmuring, with a satisfied air: "Just as I thought: *honey*!"— honey being a preservative much in vogue among mediaeval undertakers. There was no honey in the tomb of Frederick II; but the remains of *Stupor Mundi* remained relatively incorrupt. While other royal corpses hidden in the same sarcophagus had almost entirely crumbled away, the body of the stupendous Emperor still excited admiration. Wrapped in magnificent robes which had an Arabic inscription woven into the figured stuff, he wore an emerald ring, was girt with a sword and a silken girdle fastened by a silver clasp, and had boots of embroidered silk and a pair of golden spurs. The imperial orb lay beside his head, and his pearl-encrusted crown upon a leather pillow. So commanding had been his life that the report of his death was not accepted without difficulty; and a fairy story began to be bruited around—which later became attached to his grandfather Barbarossa—that Frederick, who had never died, slept deep in a mysterious cavern beneath a German mountain-range, seated at a stone table through which the tendrils of his beard grew, waiting to return to the upper air and lead back the Empire along the paths of peace and greatness.

Whereas the career of Frederick—brilliantly gifted, passionately ambitious, cruel, luxurious, headstrong—seems to contain a magnified picture both of human virtues and of human vices, subsequent monarchs merely exemplified human absurdities and petty failings. After a period of domination by the House of Anjou, against whom Sicilians took their revenge in the "Sicilian Vespers", the Kingdom of Sicily was appropriated by the Bourbons of Naples and Spain, and slumbered uneasily beneath their rule until Garibaldi's campaign made the island part of Italy. It was a peaceful, if slightly ignoble, phase; and the King of the Two Sicilies whom Nelson championed—Ferdinand III of Sicily, Ferdinand IV of Naples—was true to the dullest traditions of his type and lineage. Like many of his race, he had a boundless appetite for low company; the *lazzaroni* of Naples adored him; and their affectionate nickname, *Il Re Nasone*, has immortalised the enormous proboscis that accentuated the effect of his heavy Bourbon under-lip. Portly and slothful and immature, he was married to the daughter of Maria Theresa, Maria Carolina of Austria, an autocratic and illiberal woman, constantly haunted by the fate of her younger sister, Marie Antoinette. Friends and confidants of the King and Queen Consort were the British Ambassador and his wife, Sir William and Lady Hamilton. Among persons of extremely exalted rank, social snobbery, as Proust noted, works on individual lines; and Maria Carolina, who might well have refused her acquaintance to a respectable Englishwoman of the middle class, had become tenderly attached to the former Emmy Lyon. Extremes met, with mutual satisfaction, at their boudoir conferences. The tall imperious Austrian princess, "at once gaunt and massive", with her Hapsburg profile, her haughty carriage and her cold and glassy stare, responded to the charm of the bulky blooming English beauty whom Goethe in 1787 had proclaimed a supreme "masterpiece of the great artist—Nature", and who, even in 1798, had still something of the voluptuous appeal of a late Graeco-Roman statue. When the celebrated admiral was drawn into the beauty's web, he, too, became the Queen's protector; and, during the autumn of 1798, while the armies of the French Republic were sweeping down through Italy, and the Jacobins of Naples were rumoured to be on the point of rising, he transported the whole "august Family", with a horde of courtiers and ministers, to their southern capital. Palermo was Nelson's Capua; and there he remained, "inactive at a foreign court", till the summer months of 1800. Wildly in love yet horribly fatigued—"he seems quite dying (wrote Lady Elgin), and yet as if he had no other thought than her"—Nelson nodded through the endless festivities arranged for his own and for Lady Hamilton's benefit. Observers thought that he might be growing blind; at the card-table he would often fall asleep as he sat patiently behind his mistress' chair; yet, whenever it was a question of active life, his "infinite fire" would blaze up. No doubt he detested Palermo, its warmth and languor and incessant intrigues. But Palermo contained the beloved presence; and Emma Hamilton was the ultimate reward of a maimed, exhausted and neurotic hero.

So the parties and balls went on. "You never saw anything to equal the fuss the Queen made with Lady H.", reported Lady Elgin; and during October 1799 their Sicilian Majesties entertained the guests of honour at a gigantic Chinese fête, which was said to have cost six thousand pounds and where all the attendants were dressed in Chinese costumes. The gardens in which this fête was held must have been those of a newly-built villa called *La Favorita*. Situated in a huge park, just beneath the steep slopes of Monte Pellegrino, *La Favorita* was the creation of Marvuglia, a fashionable local architect, and deserves a place in the same gallery as George IV's marine residence. Like the Pavilion, it is both tawdry and pretty, latticed and balconied, painted pink and green, its curling Oriental eaves adorned with gilded temple-bells; and, like the Pavilion's its atmosphere is sad; for much of the effect it originally produced must have depended on the shimmer of life, on liveries and uniforms, embroidered muslins and Indian shawls, and on furniture, brightly upholstered, made of imitation bamboo. Its exoticism has faded and tarnished; but the Queen's bedchamber, though empty and naked, is an uncommonly pleasing and amusing room. Here, in the heart of Maria Carolina's *Petit Trianon*, a neo-Pompeian style of decoration has been superimposed on pseudo-Chinese; and amid the arabesques that cover the wall have been suspended medallion-portraits of her plain but numerous family. Each has an appropriate legend, testifying to the sitter's virtues and to the high esteem in which he or she was held by the sentimental Queen Consort—"*My Treasure*", "*My Jewels*", "*My Only Hope and Consolation*". Maria Carolina of the Two Sicilies was a vindictive and suspicious woman, whose carefully organised secret police arranged for the torture and execution of many harmless citizens; but this parade of family affection suggests Balmoral or Osborne. In domestic life she was clearly as effusive and sentimental as the English royal matriarch.

VI

*Taormina—the Theatre—Randazzo in Snow—Catania
and the Palazzo Biscari—Goethe's Escape from
Weimar—the Poet and the Scientist—Ruskin and
Etna—D. H. Lawrence and the Golden Snake*

Between Syracuse and Taormina, the country
grows more and more precipitous; and, as you approach and skirt
the foothills of Etna, heavy smooth white limestone rocks—
dazzlingly white, here and there, against a dark-blue sea—vanish
in prickly lava-beds, black and forbidding and dismal like the
spilt cinders of some gigantic kitchen-range. When the train
pauses at Taormina, a hotel omnibus is waiting: hotel-touts rush
forward with familiar cries, and a familiar depression descends
upon the traveller's spirit. Hotels are clustered among the
crags above—a converted convent, an improvised Moorish
palace, modestly inviting family *pensions*: you are back in the
world of obligatory pleasure, of famous views, recommended
excursions and shops selling films and coloured picture-postcards,
where the wind seems to carry a stale reek of other people's
holidays. Suggestions of expatriate talent occur in every narrow
cobbled street—a door garishly painted, a house-front cleverly
rebuilt, hinting at the presence of a pseudo-impressionist painter,
or a pair of bulldog-faced women manufacturing *batik* scarves or
seated at a hand-loom. You catch glimpses of these gallant but

unattractive figures in the little bars and eating-places. Native
inhabitants have a cautious and crafty, an expectant and yet
disillusioned, air.

Taormina has much in common with Capri—with Capri at its
most demoralised and easy-going period. For many years it was
the haunt of a German photographer—an earnestly bespectacled
and heavily bearded baron—who produced innumerable pictures
of local boys posed naked beneath olive-trees, which rich "col-
lectors" from Northern Europe delighted to purchase and bear
home. Some of his albums may still be examined; and, although
to a dispassionate eye they are singularly devoid either of
aesthetic or of erotic interest, they helped to give the town an
ambiguous prestige that twenty-five years ago had not quite
deserted it. Then its reputation for Mediterranean license continued to attract a swarm of Northern visitors. But Mussolini
decreed reforms; and, at the time of my first arrival, the same
young men who, in a certain English Tea Room, had been
accustomed to gossip and dance with admirers of their own sex,
were already circulating, just as contentedly, with romantic
middle-aged foreign ladies. Yet Taormina is not entirely corrupt;
and if, as may one day happen, the large hotels that surround it
begin to crumble and drop away—derelict swallow's-nests
dropping from a sunny wall—no doubt it will revert effortlessly
to its earlier mode of life. Even now it keeps something of its
ancient character. There is a diminutive square beyond the
miniature cathedral in which old black-cloaked men sit talking
on a low parapet, beside a fountain topped by the effigy of a
primitive she-centaur, who has womanly arms, no fore-legs but
sturdy equine back-legs; and the cathedral itself is a quiet and
delightful building, with a Renaissance statue, at once gracious
and clumsy—was it the work of a local craftsman under the spell
of Michelangelo?—representing the unfortunate female saint

from whom pagan persecutors tore her right breast. As she holds
it up in a pair of massive pincers, it resembles half a pomegranate.

At the opposite end of the town is the celebrated Greek
theatre. To be exact, it is Graeco-Roman; and during the second
half of the eighteenth century (according to the *Voyage de Naples
et de Sicile* which Fragonard and other young artists executed for
the enlightened Abbé de Non) little of it remained above ground.
Since then it has been carefully excavated; some of the columns
have been re-erected; and from its upper seats, over the pillared
proscenium, the eye may swoop through a thirty-mile expedition
along the eastern coast of Sicily, to a point where the foam-
fringed curve of the shore is broken on the horizon by the slow
descent of Etna. That magnificent mountain completes the prospect. Vast in diameter, a gigantic rugged accumulation of rock
and ash and aged snow, viewed from Taormina it seems to float
across the middle air, never vulgarly obtrusive, always nobly
dominant. Guide-books and works of reference sketch its later
history. The largest and highest volcano in Europe, "locally
known as Mongibello", Etna is thought to have been con-
tinuously active for the last three thousand years; about one
hundred and fifty eruptions have so far been chronicled; and the
most impressive disturbance it has yet achieved was in 1669,
when it overwhelmed and destroyed the city of Catania. Its
slopes (one learns from the same source) are divided into three
zones. A low lying sub-tropical belt, which grows bananas and
sugar-cane near the sea and, a little higher up, figs, oranges and
lemons, is succeeded by a second belt, between fifteen hundred
to four thousand feet, bearing olives, vines and fruit trees; and
together they form "one of the world's most densely populated
agricultural districts". Above them are the remains of Etna's
ancient forest-covering—oak and beech, juniper and birch and
pine, still emergent here and there among clumps of the golden

Etna broom: then, beyond the six-thousand foot level, are only ash and lava-rock, streaked by pinions of snow throughout the hottest summer-months.

At any season Etna is rarely beautiful, and from any point of view. But seen from Taormina it is probably loveliest; for its gradually descending eastern slope includes several separate volcanic peaks, as it slides down to the Mediterranean through three long delicate broken curves. While the sun is setting behind its flanks, these foothills stand out in a succession of dissolving planes—smoky grey and vinous purple, soft grey-blue and finally purple-black. At last its edge against the luminous sky is a solid rim of darkness; and, where the extremity of the slope plunges into the water, small fishing-boats begin to collect, each with a brilliant spark of light on the prow. During the summer, a flattened, attenuated wisp of smoke drifts above the snow-cap; but Etna is a sulky and capricious divinity—nevertheless so unmistakably divine that Empedocles' decision to die there seems not at all surprising—and during the spring it is frequently masked in cloud, and snow-drifts of formidable depth may block the roads around its foot. The road, for instance, from Randazzo to Bronte, a town which has given its name to an estate bestowed by Ferdinand IV upon his saviour, Nelson. We had climbed to Randazzo from the coastal plain, zigzagging through lava-fields and up the single streets of shuttered silent villages; and as we advanced, the atmosphere of spring receded, till many miles short of our objective we reached an Alpine wilderness. The surrounding landscape was buried in snow; the streets of Randazzo itself were clogged with heaps of icy slush. Snow-water dripped from the eaves; and, deserting my companions, I explored the icy cavern of an immense deserted black-columned church, which smelt of faith and old incense-smoke, but also of solitude and gloom and poverty. Outside, black-cloaked, black-hooded passers-by had appeared remote and hostile. In the church, however, I was soon joined by a short effusive young man, who, politely refusing to leave my side, and introducing me, one after another, to various chance-met friends of his, presently led me down snowy lanes to a local drinking-place, where we ordered some bottles of sharp but comforting Etna wine. I there learned that he was a former prisoner-of-war, and that—unlike the acquaintance we afterwards made at Ragusa, who confessed that he was sorry but he could not love the English, since prison-camp life (thumping his heart) had done something to him *al cuore*—he had spent the happiest period of his existence around an English farmyard. What a delightful country, particularly near York! The wine was strong, though not very good; the kitchen shone with oil-cloth; and, explaining that he had had an English *amica*, he soon asked me to admire her portrait—the photograph of a stout, featureless, bespectacled girl, whose name, he said, was Dorothy. But Dorothy, he added, was a dream of the past, the exquisite Circean apparition every Odysseus leaves behind him. He had returned to his Randazzo-Ithaka, and was today a married man.

Foiled in our attempts to circumnavigate Etna—lorry-drivers assured us that the next ten miles of the road were utterly impassable—we turned on our tracks and retreated to Catania. With the exception of Palermo, this is the worldliest and most metropolitan of Sicilian cities; for not only is it populous and large, but it has a native aristocracy of unusual size and consequence. Proust would have appreciated the titles they bear; and he might have been amused to note that Sicilian princes, who are also barons, in common with M. de Charlus prefer the baronial style, as having a more ancient, hence more distinguished, origin. Owners of these resplendent names, their overcoats in Southern fashion draped across their shoulders, fill the rather dingy

downstairs-rooms of Catania's biggest hotel. They share their
compatriots' appetite for endless masculine conversation; and "Do
you know what they are all of them talking about?" enquired
our Catanian ally, who, though a representative of the same caste,
had a considerably broader and less uncultivated range of interests:
"Every one you see here is talking about *women*". It did not
mean that many of the talkers would not go home to bed alone;
but women were the mainstay of talk as were politics, the crops
or prices in other social milieus. They devoted themselves to the
discussion of sex from an abstract love of the subject . . .

Most of the famous families of Catania (to whom our informant's account of their conversation was possibly neither
just nor kind) besides villas in the country, still maintain their
town houses. Among the best is the Palazzo Biscari, which has
a dignified classical entrance-court and a garden-balcony looking
out to sea, sculptured in a richly exuberant local version of the
Baroque mannerism. The ante-chambers of these palaces are
frequently frescoed or hung with huge decorative maps of
the family's ancestral estates; and the portraits exhibited in other
rooms show an imposing, if slightly alarming, range of late-
seventeenth-century or eighteenth-century forebears, stolid personages, usually Spanish in type, their portentous patrician
gravity set off by the weight of Bourbon lips and jowls. But the
finest feature of the Palazzo Biscari is its lofty ballroom. Richly
painted, glimmering with looking-glass panels, it is paved with
glazed Spanish tiles of green and azure and vivid yellow. At the
end of the room, an apsidal niche once contained the canopied
state bed in which princesses of the house received ceremonial
visits a few days after child-birth. The painted ceiling forms an
incomplete dome, pierced at the centre by a galleried lantern;
and in the lantern, which is approached from the gallery beyond
by a Rococo corkscrew staircase, the orchestra used to play,

perched twenty or thirty feet above the assembled dancers' heads. Looking down, the musicians in the roof may have imagined that they surveyed a living, moving parterre, as the embroidered shoulders and sleeves of the men and the wide brocaded skirts of the women swung rhythmically to and fro on the multi-coloured arabesques of the floral pavement underfoot.

Goethe visited the Palazzo Biscari on May 3rd 1787. There he inspected a "large collection of marble and bronze figures, vases and all sorts of such-like antiques", especially admiring a torso of Zeus, now relegated to the civic museum housed in the mediaeval castle, and was hospitably entertained by the Prince—a man of great culture, though his portrait suggests that he must have resembled a Giant Sloth—who, in spite of the thefts committed by previous visitors, as a "singular mark of his confidence" showed the poet his collection of coins. The Princess, his mother, was no less gracious, and "with her own hands" opened the cabinet in which she kept some exquisite specimens of Sicilian amber, wrought into a variety of urns and cups, ranging from translucent to entirely opaque, and from waxen-hued to honey-coloured, and thence "through all possible shades of a deep yellow, to the most beautiful hyacinthian red". Goethe's visit was an important episode in Sicilian literary history. It was also a crucial period of the writer's career. Poised on the threshold of middle age, he was a fugitive not only from Weimar, where he had performed the duties of a laborious court-official since 1775, but from the whole burden of spiritual conformity that life at Weimar represented. A modern essayist has written an eloquent appreciation* of the "sketch which Johann Tischbein made in one of the bedrooms of a Roman inn, while Goethe was leaning out of the window and looking down on to the street below. It is a graceful, a forceful and a noble back . . . Had

* *Mainly On The Air* by Sir Max Beerbohm (published by William Heineman).

Napoleon been there to see it, he would have murmured, as . . .
he did when he saw Goethe face to face at Weimar in later years,
'Voila un homme!' It is moreover the back of a man rapt in
contemplation . . . a man avidly observing, learning, storing up.
He is wearing slippers, he has not yet put on his waistcoat nor
buttoned his breeches at the knees. His toilet can wait. His
passionate curiosity cannot. It is an intimate, as significant a
portrait as ever was made of one man by another''.

Having spent more than two months in the study of Rome—
from November 1st to February 21st—where he conceived the
original plan of his erotic *Roman Elegies*, was portrayed by the
attentive Tischbein wearing a broad-brimmed hat and a classic
mantle reclining at his ease among the ruins of the Campagna,
and renewed his own early interest in the art of draughtsman-
ship, Goethe turned to the South and, from Naples, set sail for
Palermo on the 29th of March. Rome had proved an intoxicating
experience—an adventure so eagerly awaited that, until he had
passed under the Porto del Popolo, he scarcely dared admit, even
to himself, whither he was hurrying and often had fears that he
might somehow never reach his goal. Yet, although transfigured
by the impressions he received, released from his previous
spiritual load and irradiated by a magnificent influx of fresh
creative energy, his powers of assimilation and critical dis-
crimination were at no time overwhelmed: he remained the
master of the sensations he enjoyed, the meticulous observer as
well as the adventurer, an aspiring scientist as well as an artist.
Common sense never failed to come to his aid; and when, during
the passage to Sicily, the sea became rough and he was threatened
with an attack of sickness, he immediately adopted practical
measures, retired to his cabin, took up a horizontal position
(which he knew to be the best one) and, having decided to
refrain from all nourishment except white bread and red wine,

94

was soon comfortable and calm enough to get to work on an unfinished manuscript. The first two acts of *Tasso* continued to absorb him; and presently he was again on deck, whence, extending his telescope, he watched the progress of an unusually large turtle.

He also gazed with delight at a shoal of dolphins and noted how, as these carefree creatures accompanied the ship, weaving their way through the transparent swell and often leaping clear of it, along their fins and spine-ridged bodies the light changed from gold to green and then from green to gold. The same blend of practical acumen and poetic ardour appears in his description of the months that followed. A man of genius is not always the most impassioned of descriptive sightseers. Less talented travellers may affect a more romantic attitude; for the possessor of genius frequently resembles the owner of an elaborate, costly and delicately organised camera who, while his friends are content to gaze and dream, is preoccupied with the mysterious mechanism of the instrument he is carrying round, and with the importance of focusing it correctly and making use of it worthily. A sense of responsibility seldom ceases to haunt him; and Goethe's sense of the duty he owed his genius—his constant desire to increase his knowledge and employ his intelligence to the greatest possible advantage—gives his record, now and then, a strangely arid and prosaic turn. In Venice he had already passed as much time meditating "upon the structure of cuttlefish and the habits of crabs" as musing upon the Grand Canal; and in Palermo, beneath the dense, almost tropical foliage of the Botanical Gardens—a perfect setting for an imaginative work he contemplated about the love-story of Nausikaa—he was distracted from the luxurious absorption of scents and colours and southern sunlight by his "old fancy" concerning *Urphänomene*, his theory of "basic forms in which are contained all the possibilities

of development of any given species". Under its influence
the Gardens of Alkinous vanished. "Might I not discover the
primordial plant among all these numerous specimens? Some
such there must be! For, otherwise how am I able to determine
that this or that form is a plant unless they are all formed after
one original type?" And, discarding his poetic projects as if
they were a hat or cloak, he strode busily botanising up and
down the alley-ways.

Nor was Goethe's feeling for beauty or interest in antiquity
always that of the modern world. True, he admired the Palazzo
Zisa; but he did not visit, or was not informed of the existence
of, the Capella Palatina; while the charming circular fountain in
the Piazza Pretoria, created by two Florentine artists in the year
1555 and afterwards brought from a Tuscan villa to adorn a
Sicilian public place, with its dimpled goddesses and nymphs and
tritons and surround of grimacing animal-heads, merely struck
him as a clumsy, over-ornamented and still half-barbarous monument. Nearly as deplorable as Prince Palagonia's efforts! The
Prince's country-house at Bagheria astonished and disgusted him.*
To his own cult of classical repose nothing could have been more
antipathetic than the monsters and pygmies, the interior decoration of antlers and spears, looking-glass, marble-inlays and
mosaics of broken Chinese porcelain capriciously glued together
to form fantastic wall-coverings, with which that perverse
virtuoso preferred to live surrounded. Besides, the whole place
was disorderly and ruinous. "Here (he noted) we find an
Egyptian figure, built into the wall, a fountain without water, a
monument, vases stuck around in no sort of order, statues
designedly laid upon their noses . . . The ground is, for the most
part, overgrown with grass. Here . . . are marble urns with

* An admirable account of the Villa Palagonia is to be found in the opening
chapter of Sacheverell Sitwell's *Southern Baroque Art.*

strange scrolls and foliations, collected by his father: dwarfs and other abortions of the later epoch . . . One even comes upon an arbour, propped up with ancient vases, and stone scrolls of various shapes."

He was interested, however, in the eccentric Prince himself, a man as extraordinary as Beckford, as shudderingly sensitive to the vulgar contacts of the real world. While he conversed with a Palermitan shop-keeper, Goethe was suddenly accosted by a tall and well-dressed menial who thrust before him a silver salver on which were a number of copper coins and a few pieces of silver; and, when he enquired what this demand for charity meant, the shop-keeper, "with a very significant mien, and somewhat stealthily", pointed to a lean, haggard, elderly gentleman, apparelled in the height of fashion, "walking with great dignity and indifference through the dung and dirt". It was the Prince Palagonia, explained his acquaintance, taking up a collection to ransom Christian slaves in Barbary. With a sword at his side and his hat beneath his arm, frizzled and powdered, wearing a silken vest, neat shoes and jewelled shoe-buckles, "the old man walked on calmly and sorrowfully", and "all eyes were directed towards him". "Palagonian", nevertheless, remained the word that Goethe employed to denote extravagant bad taste; and, since Palermo—particularly among its churches, "in which even the Jesuit's love of show and finery is surpassed"—showed many buildings, both religious and secular, of a far too Palagonian kind, notwithstanding the charm of the Botanical Gardens and the splendour of the sea and mountains he set out willingly enough on an exploration of the remote interior. From Alcamo, a "quiet town", he reached Segesta during late April. The incomplete temple, he found, occupied a "singular" site, commanding a "very distant and extensive view of the land, but . . . only just a corner of the sea". There was scarcely a

G

house in view; yet the landscape that he surveyed impressed him as "well cultivated", brooding in an atmosphere of "melancholy fertility". The tops of the flowering thistles were alive with countless butterflies, and the "wild fennel stood here from eight to nine feet high, dry and withered of the last year's growth . . . A shrill wind whistled through the columns as if through a wood, and screaming birds of prey hovered around the pediments".

From Segesta, by way of Castel Vetrano and Sciacca, he pushed on to Girgenti; and there, in the living-room of a private house, separated only by a green curtain from the members of a large family who were busily occupied manufacturing macaroni "of the whitest and smallest kind", he discovered a congenial resting-place. Sitting down beside the pretty children, he had the whole process of manufacture explained to him in careful detail, and how the finished product was made from the "finest and hardest wheat called *grano forte*". Naturally the ruins called for a scholarly tour; the porous columns, he observed, had at some time been encrusted with "dazzling white gypsum"—or had the gypsum been supplied at a later period to repair the stone's porosity? But he was equally concerned with geological notes and with the methods used in Sicily for the cultivation of flax and beans: with gleaming scraps of political opinion—"great hatred is felt there against the French, because they have made peace with the people of Barbary": even, if he had nothing better to do, with watching "our excellent *vetturino*" relish his meals of "raw artichokes and the turnip-cabbage"—vegetables, he felt bound to add, which seemed much more succulent than they were at home. Then Kniep, his artist companion, carried him up on to the sacred rock. They looked out over the sea beyond, and Kniep bade him remark the broad streak of cloud which bordered the horizon. That, he said, indicated the coast of Africa. Sunset was near; and an immense rainbow, resting one foot on Sicily, advanced its luminous arc into the far distance. Probably its other foot rested on Malta; and Goethe dallied with the agreeable notion that the "attractive force of the two islands" might thus be gaily manifested.

From Segesta they travelled to Caltanisetta and the ancient citadel of Castrogiovanni; and, as they ascended the flank of the acropolis, Goethe had leisure to remark that the "rock consisted of muschelkalk", large calcined shells being heaped together beside the road. On the plains below the bean was in full blossom; but at the former Enna they passed a miserable night, for rain was beating down and the stone-flagged room they occupied had shutters but no glazed windows. More hospitable and entertaining were Catania and Taormina; and, of all the Sicilian towns that had harboured Goethe, Taormina pleased him most. As nightingales sang under his balcony, the dormant poet re-emerged. The sky was clear. He was refreshed by the smell of the sea: roses and oleanders blossomed in the gardens, amid flowering orange and lemon groves: an indefinable unearthly radiance suffused orchards, rocks and headlands, and gave the smoking cone of the great volcano itself a friendly, unforbidding look. What finer place to write of the daughter of Alkinous, as he had planned to do at Palermo when his imagination had been distracted by the delusive idea of "basic forms"— to go back to the youth of humanity, the morning world of Mediterranean? And, opening his copy of the *Odyssey*, inspired by deep hope and "incredible interest" Goethe began to re-read . . .

Such, with its glimpses of beans and butterflies, of curious stones picked up by the road and of the beautifully coloured mosses that flourished on volcanic slag, of Prince Palagonia in the streets of Palermo and some horrible noisy Englishmen described to him at Catania by the waiter of the *Golden Lion*, is Goethe's account of his escape to Sicily. Since that period wave after wave of northern invaders has broken on the Sicilian coasts —writers and scholars and fashionable persons, hedonists in search of illicit pleasure as well as the vast dowdy throng of water-colour-painting English ladies whose camp-stools and easels used, between the Wars, to dot the landscape around Girgenti. It is to be regretted that Byron, who had intended to visit the island with his friends the Oxfords—his mistress, the seductive "Aspasia", her lovely children, "the Harleian Miscellany", and her negligible and neglected husband—should have cancelled his passage at the last moment: and that Newman, who arrived in the 'fifties, was so preoccupied with interior conflicts that he seldom turned his gaze outward and gives only a bare mention of the places that he passed through. But John Ruskin, never again to venture thus far South, appeared in the Spring of 1874. At the time he was still obsessed by his desperate infatuation for Rose La Touche and lived in a kind of waking dream, faithful to his visionary cult of the slender, fair-haired Irish girl, who had teased and encouraged and continued to hold him off, till self-control and sanity itself seemed on the verge of foundering. In Ruskin's nature the claims of the sensuous and the demands of the spiritual life had long been fighting an indecisive battle: his intense appreciation of the beauty of the flesh and the world was in perpetual revolt against his ingrained puritanism: but his happier impulses were constantly checked by a conviction of sin and a sense of deep unworthiness. Now, as he grew older, his intimations of evil began to materialise in strangely concrete images: he saw a "Storm Cloud" spread across Europe, which blighted the radiance of the clearest skies, stained the purity of the loneliest lakes, and had even defiled and diminished his beloved Alpine glaciers. Yet there were intervals when the nightmare lifted; and rarely did it lift so long as during the few exquisite Spring days he spent at rest in Sicily.

In Naples his sense of the degradation of mankind had become a form of moral torture. It was, he declared, "certainly the most disgusting place in Europe"; for it combined "the vice of Paris with the misery of Dublin and the vulgarity of New York", "the most loathsome nest of human caterpillars I was ever forced to stay in,—a hell with all the devils imbeciles". But the shadow of the "Storm Cloud" did not quite extend to Sicily. At the end of April he was in Taormina; and, very early on the morning of the 26th, having hurriedly dressed by the light of dawn, the tall, thin, weather-beaten, whiskered Englishman, with his piercing blue eyes and carefully informal clothes, reached a "little lonely campo in front of a chapel, looking down, fifteen hundred feet, to the seashore, and across to Etna, whose cone rises in one long sweep . . ." From the crest of the mountain white smoke was ascending two thousand feet higher "in a perfectly vertical column . . . with a . . . visible motion like that of ordinary slow smoke . . . Where the sun touched the base of the smoke without descending to the mountain summit, it was literally the Israelite pillar of Fire and Cloud". That dawn was the "most awful thing I ever yet saw, in heaven or earth". But, no sooner had its rosy flush touched the snows of the mountain itself than—as if to recall him to the disharmony of real life—"the belfry of the chapel beside me broke into a discordant jangle of deep-toned bells . . . the bells very fine and solemn in tone, but dreadfully painful from the discordant and violent ringing". Even here there were men to resent and despise; no doubt the Sicilians belonged to the same disgusting breed as the degraded Neapolitans; "the quantity of horrible annoyance of moral as well as bodily nerve one has to bear sometimes from this entirely neglected and lost people . . .

cannot be told; it makes me angry and sorrowful to a degree I never was yet . . ." And once again Ruskin transferred his scrutiny to the rose-flushed mountain crest: " . . . Think that from the earliest dawn of Greek life that cone has been the centre of tradition and passion as relating to the gods of strength and darkness (Proserpine's city is in the mid-island, but in full sight of Etna), and you may fancy what a wild dream of incredible, labyrinthine wonder it is to me".

Some fifty years later a very different Englishman—different yet with some curious points of resemblance—came to rest for a while in Taormina. D. H. Lawrence may well have abominated Ruskin, if he had ever troubled to read his works; but, as I have suggested elsewhere, "both in their poetic brilliance and their illogicality", the author of *Sons and Lovers* and the author of *Praeterita* very often reveal an unexpected kinship. Each was a puritan yet a passionate lover of life: each railed at his fellow men, yet fretted furiously at the mysterious barrier that seemed to keep him isolated: each was a poet who longed to preach and teach, and who projected his sense of frustration into a multitude of dramatic images. Lawrence's stay in Sicily did not outlast a summer, and he had originally intended to settle not at Taormina but at Girgenti. Thither he went searching for a house; but, acutely sensitive to the mood of a place, he could find no peace or comfort there. Local influences were particularly unpropitious; and friends who accompanied him on his house-hunting visit have told me of the strange phenomena that his mere arrival seemed to cause. Though not unused to the ways of *forestieri*, the inhabitants turned suddenly hostile; and, while Lawrence was walking outside the town, in a small circular green hat he had brought from Southern Germany, a gang of sulphur-miners with cries of "*Tedesco*" threw some random stones at him. Whereupon Lawrence biblically cursed the place, and a violent tempest sprang up, full of dust and scraps of paper, sweeping the writer himself through the interstices of a cactus-hedge. Not until he had arrived at Taormina did he regain his peace of mind; and it was at Taormina, on the terrace of his villa, with Etna sleepily smoking above the torrid July hush, that he encountered the golden snake, afterwards described in one of his most delightful prose-poems, which glided from the bowels of the earth to sip the water of a garden-tank, then glided back—a symbol of the infernal powers—into the heat and darkness from which it had come. Lawrence's poem may be paralleled in many of Ruskin's prose-digressions. Each felt the unending conflict between the light and dark gods. Neither of them, so long as he lived, torn between flesh and spirit, could achieve a mental equipoise.

VII

A Sicilian Koré—Greece and the Middle East—
Landscape and Art—The beginning of the road
—Hellenic dawn and Hellenistic decline—The
Byzantine revival—At the end of the journey

T HE ONLY RELIC I brought home from Sicily
was a curving fragment of terra-cotta, some six inches long by
four-and-a-half inches broad, the gift of a generous Palermitan
friend in whose house I had admired it. Dug up in the fields near
Segesta or Himera, this warm-coloured scrap of baked earth,
stripped of the smooth layer of pigment that must at one time
have covered its surface, retains a texture sufficiently rough to
suggest its earthy origins. It evokes the physical substance of its
native landscape—calcareous rocks, bare mountain-slopes, dry
fields among the olive-trees; but on the gritty stuff of which it
was moulded human emotion and human ingenuity have left
their moving imprint. Mind has interpenetrated and transfigured
matter, so that a lump of yellowish clay, squeezed and stroked
between the palms of an anonymous local artist whose finger-
marks you can still observe where they kneaded out the cheek
from within, has blossomed into that faint mysterious smile which
irradiates many sculptured faces of the fifth and sixth centuries.
My fragment probably belongs to the sixth. Part of the head of a
humble votive statue, it includes the whole of the chin and mouth

18 *ETNA FROM TAORMINA*

19   *TAORMINA: Cathedral and fountain*

20   *RANDAZZO: A Mediaeval Street*

21 *SIXTH-CENTURY SICILIAN TERRA-COTTA: Fragment of a votive statue*

22   THE CATHEDRAL OF CEFALU: *Interior*

and nose, the right eye, a triangle of forehead and a wide downward-sweeping band of curled or tightly braided tresses, with some indications of a small and sensitive ear and of the serpentine locks that escaped beneath ear-lobe. The complete figure may have stood a little over three feet tall. The right forearm, with the elbow close to the side, was, no doubt, extended.

For this is a *Kore*, a sacred Maiden, member of the same delightful sisterhood as those maidens one admires in the museums at Athens. Unlike them, it lacks the distinction of an accomplished masterpiece, and its creator was presumably an industrious artisan who manufactured such clay effigies to supply a thriving pilgrim-trade. Yet what he may have lacked in individual, he made up in racial, genius, working as he did during a period of history when the inspiration of the Hellenic races was just beginning to take definite shape. It is unmistakably an archaic head; and the features he designed follow the strict conventions of archaic beauty. The nose is a shade longer than we should expect to find in a statue of the Periclean epoch: the narrow eye, very lightly modelled, has an attractive, almost Eastern slant. But there is nothing impersonal about the face as a whole, nothing static in the charm of its contours which constantly change and take on new expression, according to the angle at which it is placed or the movement of the lamp by which it is viewed. For all its simplicity it is extraordinarily alive: for all the vague sweetness of its smile, which waxes or wanes as one turns it from side to side, it has a look of subtle eagerness. The mouth has an especial fascination, firmly indented at the corners, yet running up towards the cheeks in the most delicate of gentle curves. That smile has been well described by a contemporary classical scholar. Discussing the "curious intense expression", the appealingly "vivid look", of some of the archaic statues found on the

Acropolis, he concludes that it is "expressive of nothing so much as of the plain fact of their animate existence . . . Later ages could afford to . . . refine, at least to complicate, the first sculptor's problem, which was, quite simply, to make a living man out of a piece of stone. The archaic artist was less ambitious. His problem was to create a personality rather than a character . . . He was . . . content if he could find the particular form in which . . . the general fact of existence must be clothed . . . And that is why archaic art, whatever its limitations, is rarely dull; it is the proof of a conviction that, through the workings of his personality, the artist may make the world of inanimate matter burn with the fire of life".*

Thus the smile may be interpreted as a smile of triumph. Yet it is something more than the triumphant assertion of their own animate existence that gives the products of the early Greek sculptor their peculiar and inimitable charm. Compare them, for instance, with some of the sculptures of the Middle East. There, too, you admire the look of intentness; and few statues are so compact of vitality—of energy of a certain limited, but none the less beguiling, kind—as works produced in Southern Babylonia two thousand years before Christ. I am thinking particularly of the portraits of the Sumerian city-governor, generally called Gudea, of which one is preserved in the Louvre and another in the British Museum. In the Louvre Gudea is seated and wears a close-fitting lambswool cap; while in the British Museum he stands bare-headed and the light falls directly on his egg-shaped shaven skull. Each statue folds its hands, with a firm, authoritative gesture, just above the midriff. Both have a resolute and dauntless air; and, thanks to the magical processes of art, the four-thousand-year-old Sumerian official still addresses us in a language

* *Archaic Marble Sculpture From The Acropolis*, by Humfry Payne and Gerard Mackworth Young (published by Cresset Press).

undistorted by the passage of time. He speaks of wisdom and power and wealth, of self-satisfaction as solid as his smoothly muscled shoulders. We can be sure that he respected and served the gods; but nothing in heaven or earth unduly stirred or troubled him. He was unconscious of the threat of the future. But—how many of the onlookers can say as much?—he embellished and enjoyed his own age.

That, I imagine, would be the tone of Gudea's voice; and as comfortably matter-of-fact was his territorial background. Behind him stretches the interminable river-plain beneath a sky discoloured by heat. Here and there rises a pyramidal sanctuary, from which in a vertical column wreathes up the smoke of sacrifices; and among these sacred mounds, extending to the horizon, appears an occasional walled city, with flocks and herds being driven home through the dust and straight irrigation-ditches ruled across the palm-groves. A drab, friendly, prosaic landscape. How different is the mood evoked by the smallest fragment of early Greek sculpture! The life that quickens it is not the "life of the spirit", but belongs to a world in which flesh and spirit merge into the same pattern—or, rather, in which spiritual and corporeal impulses have not yet begun to grow apart. Here the mind still delights in the body, and the body is still eloquent of the stirrings of the mind within. Divine beings are content with a human guise; and the familiar landscape is scattered with reminders of divinity, which confer an animate charm on trees and rocks and mountain-torrents. If man himself is intensely alive, so is the accustomed earth he treads, the mountain-slopes that enclose his fields, the dark-blue "unharvested" sea that shimmers below the cliff-edge.

Early Greek art has a quality of freshness unknown to other races and ages. How it materialised—through precisely what combination of ethnic or geographical causes—is a question yet unanswered by the archaeologist or the art-critic. But we cannot discount the influence of the country it sprang from; for no other corner of the globe, in proportion to its size, has an imaginative effect more powerful, a spiritual character more strongly marked. No other country has been endowed with at once so soft and so rich a light. Hills, that appear rugged and formless while rain is falling or the sun is hidden, suddenly re-emerge, when the sky is unveiled, in crystalline ridges of translucent colour—the deep violet of the hills round Athens, behind Sparta the russets and purples of the foothills of Taygetos, the lively greens and sub-marine blues of the enormous Macedonian plain. And, if the landscape is pre-eminently rich in legends, nowhere else do the creatures of legend seem more real and comprehensible. I remember, for instance, how during a visit to Delphi, as we stood under the crags of Parnassos with the wide-winged eagles of Zeus wheeling slowly overhead, a friend accompanying us, who is a professional singer, decided to try a high note. An echo replied from the precipices of the sacred mountain; and Echo, the classical nymph, haunter of solitary places, leapt into the mind almost before the sound had died away. A second and third note strengthened the illusion. Now the nymph's call came closer to us: now it had receded. Now there appeared to be a per-ceptible hesitation—a mocking pause, a second of surprise or doubt—between the note and the returning cry. Its timbre had an extraordinary wildness and strangeness; and instinctively one looked up at the rocks above for some momentary brilliant manifestation of a nymphean face and body . . .

I have wandered far from my original theme; but many of the richest aspects of the Sicilian background are connected with its Grecian youth; and it is there that the traveller who wished to obtain a really comprehensive view of the island would, no doubt, begin his survey. None of the Greek sites is difficult to reach, Segesta being a few hours' drive from Palermo, which is, of course, linked by rail with Syracuse and Agrigento; while Selinunte, the furthest and most destroyed, is just off the main coastal road running to Trapani and Marsala. On the way he will journey through different periods and through landscapes despoiled or reshaped by the influence of different races—past Baroque churches and Rococo country houses, along coastlines gay and luxuriant, or bleached and pitiably eroded by a thousand years of neglect and misuse. But, once arrived, if he retains even the remnants of a classical education, he will notice that he is on familiar ground, and recollection after recollection will seem to slip into its proper place. Part of Odysseus' voyage is supposed to have skirted Sicily; and he will find caves that might have harboured the Cyclops, and creeks to which Nausikaa might have driven down her mule-cart. Or he will remember the early vase-paintings. How easy to people these headlands and heights, these winding rocky paths, with the long-robed charioteers and spear-carrying men-at-arms of some black-figured wine jar! He may think, too, of the fragmentary verses left behind them by the lyric poets—of Alcman describing the aged ceryl, that "sea-purple bird of the Spring" which flies over the "flower of the wave" among attendant halcyons: or Sappho, writing of flowers and orchards and of the slow descent of the moon which shines across her empty bed.

It was to this vernal period of thought and feeling that Theocritus of Syracuse looked back from his Alexandrian exile. But the Sicily he evoked was already largely make-believe, as the cosmopolitan rule of Alexander's successors prepared the world for the deadening bureaucratic uniformity of the Roman Empire. Sicily bore the full weight of Roman strength and Roman greed, its ancient cities becoming museum-pieces, admiringly visited but frequently plundered by the custodian-power; its native artists, laborious provincial hacks. Classical art was killed by satiety, by the uncontrolled exuberance of the qualities that had once sustained it; for, just as an intense delight in the beauty of the flesh irradiates the work of the early vase-painter and sculptor, so an excessive preoccupation with the fleshly envelope finally overwhelmed and obliterated the vision that had directed their skill. The Hellenic artist had been an animist, and the master-pieces that he produced are equally sensuous and spiritual; whereas the Hellenistic craftsman dwells wearisomely upon the sensual surface of things—the obvious charm of a cherubic Eros, the heavy breasts and dimpled flanks of the Landolina Goddess of Love. His was the materialism that spills over into commonplace realism or encourages the vulgarest forms of pictorial senti-mentality.

If Sicily illustrates the growth of Greek art, and contains many specimens of Hellenistic and Graeco-Roman decadence, it may also help to explain how the creative impulse broke free. The Byzantine artist was still a Greek, in so far as he spoke Greek and, probably with little enough reason, believed that he was of Grecian descent; and, while the Roman structure was crumbling and disappearing, he completed the cyclical process begun on the Greek mainland during the sixth and fifth centuries. Than the type of expression that he perfected, few arts in world-history have been more carefully divorced from the appeal of the flesh. Here the human body has become a cipher, a symbol, robed or uniformed, in the transcendent drama of the Divine Purpose. The human face is itself an abstraction; and, though one example of a Byzantine joke survives—a somewhat ponderous pleasantry at the expense of a prince of the church who was much too fond of horse-breeding—it was an art that seldom condescended to smile, but reflected the universe in a mood of fearful seriousness. The love of God was equivalent to the fear of God, personified

in the lineaments of Christ the dreadful All-Ruler. Replacing
the gaiety and grace of the individual subject was the splendour
of the courtly ministrants who circled around the Divine Throne.

So a traveller who has seen the Greek temples should make his
next halt among the Byzantine monuments clustered on the north
coast. Palermo is an exceedingly agreeable city, to which in the
foregoing notes I fear that I may have done less than justice. It has
good hotels—comparatively rare in Sicily—including the *Hotel
des Palmes* where Wagner completed *Parsifal*, one tolerable
restaurant and several pleasant main streets. The Quattro Canti,
at which four streets join, is an excellent piece of early-
seventeenth-century town planning, "embellished with columns
and statues" in the year 1609 by an ambitious Spanish viceroy.
But its Norman-Byzantine churches, as I have already suggested,
are Palermo's chief distinction—the incomparable Capella
Palatina, S. Maria dell'Ammiraglio, S. Giovanni degli Eremiti,
which possesses a delightful flowery Moorish cloister beneath a
group of red-painted Moorish domes like bisected Dutch cheeses,
and the Cathedral of Monreale which looks down from the hills
beyond. As impressive is the Cathedral of Cefalu, a romantic
town below a perpendicular crag in which an English occultist,
Alastair Crowley, once practised magical rites and entertained
his band of disciples. Everywhere the background of golden
mosaic sets off the terrible looming features of Christos Pantokrator: every detail speaks of divine authority and human
insignificance. The wind that blows from these crags of the spirit
is perhaps slightly too sharp for modern lungs; and, though one
may not share the prejudices of a well-known English literary
personage who recently refused to enter the Cathedral of Auxerre
but chose to remain in the square outside, wrapped in a thick
overcoat and heavy clouds of Palinuroid gloom, we have many of
us, confronted by the unearthly splendour of Gothic or

Byzantine art, found ourselves hankering after a warmer and less inhuman spiritual climate. That again Sicily can provide. Serpotta and the architects of Noto were humanists in the great tradition; and amid the masterpieces they gave to their island a traveller may do well to conclude his expedition through the Sicilian Spring. Every rewarding journey is a journey in search of oneself; and at Noto, with its harmony, its golden solidity and sense of human dignity, he may feel that he is re-discovering a self whom he is not ashamed to recognise.

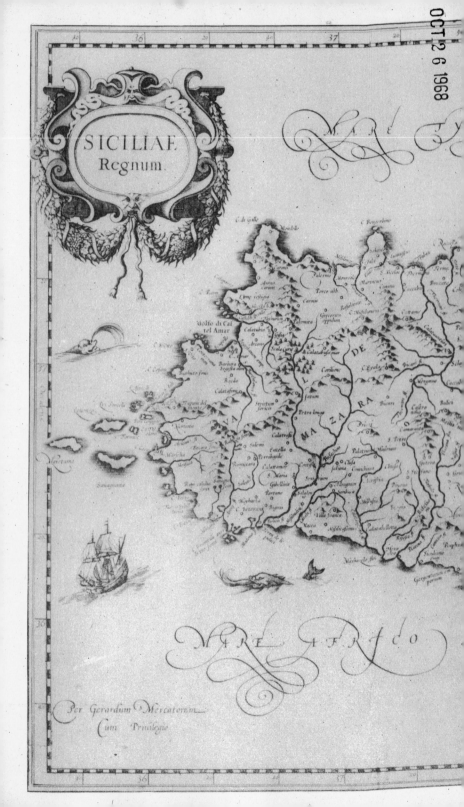

SICILIAE. Regnum.

MARE *T*

DE *L* *MAZARA* *VA*

MARE AFRICO

Per Gerardum Mercatorem Cum Privilegio